Insecure Inner Jerk

Austyn ingram

Published by Austyn ingram, 2024.

INSECURE INNER JERK

First edition. May 8, 2024.

ISBN: 979-8224913169

Written by Austyn ingram.

Table of Contents

Part 1: meet your inner jerk (and learn to laugh at it)

Chapter 1: The brain's bizarre bias

Why your inner voice is a drama queen (and how to make It sing showtunes)

Have you ever noticed how your brain seems to have a built-in negativity bias? It's like you have a tiny Gremlin perched on your shoulder, constantly whispering doubts, fears, and worst-case scenarios. It's enough to make you wonder if your brain is actively trying to sabotage your happiness.

Fear not, fellow negativity-battlers! This isn't a personal attack from your brain. It's actually a fascinating evolutionary quirk that dates back to the days of our caveman ancestors. Back in the good ol' days, when saber-toothed tigers roamed the land and your lunch could literally try to eat you, negativity bias was a survival tool.

Think about it: focusing on the negative was crucial for our ancestors. It helped them spot danger quickly, like noticing that rustling in the bushes might be a hungry lion instead of a friendly squirrel. It also helped them avoid making mistakes, like remembering not to eat that bright red berry that might just be poison in disguise.

But here's the thing: our brains haven't quite gotten the memo that we're not living in the jungle anymore. While avoiding lions and poisonous berries is still a good idea, our negativity bias has gotten a bit out of control.

It's like our brains are still stuck in survival mode, constantly scanning for threats, even when there aren't any. This leads to a whole lot of unnecessary worry, anxiety, and self-doubt. It's like having a smoke detector that goes off every time you toast a bagel, making you jumpy and stressed even though there's no real fire.

So, why does our brain still hold onto this negativity bias even though we don't need it as much anymore? Well, it turns out, our brains are creatures of habit. They like things the way they are, even if it's not always the most helpful.

It's like trying to teach your grandma how to use a smartphone – it takes time, patience, and a whole lot of repetition.

But here's the good news: just like you can teach your grandma how to use technology, you can also teach your brain to break free from its negativity bias. It's not easy, but it's definitely possible.

Here are a few ways to start:

1. Befriend your gremlin: Instead of fighting your inner negativity, try befriending it. Give it a name, like Debbie Downer Dave or Melvin the Misery Magnet. This will help you separate yourself from your negativity and see it as an external force, not something inherent to you.

2. Catch yourself in the act: Pay attention to when your negativity bias kicks in. Are you focusing on the negative aspects of a situation? Are you comparing yourself to others? Once you become aware of your negative thoughts, you can start to challenge them.

3. Flip the script: When you catch yourself thinking negatively, try to reframe the situation in a more positive light. Instead of focusing on what you don't have, focus on what you do have. Instead of dwelling on your mistakes, focus on the lessons you learned.

4. Surround yourself with positivity: Spend time with people who make you feel good about yourself. Read books and listen to music that uplift you. Immerse yourself in positive environments that will help you drown out the negativity.

5. Be kind to yourself: Remember, you're not alone in this. Everyone deals with negativity from time to time. Don't beat yourself up for having negative thoughts. Instead, be kind to yourself and accept that it's a normal part of life.

Breaking free from your negativity bias is a journey, not a destination. There will be setbacks along the way, but with time and effort, you can learn to retrain your brain and cultivate a more positive outlook on life. Remember, you have the power to control your thoughts, and ultimately, your happiness.

So, go forth and conquer your inner Gremlin! Turn that negativity into humor, that doubt into confidence, and that worry into excitement. Life is too short to spend it listening to a Drama Queen in your head. Let's replace the negativity with showtunes, laughter, and a whole lot of "woo-hoos!"

Now, you might be thinking, "But wait, doesn't focusing on the positive all the time make you naïve and unprepared for the real world?"

To that, I say, "Nonsense!" While it's true that a healthy dose of caution and realism is important, there's a big difference between being prepared and being a pessimistic worrywart.

Think of it like this: you're planning a camping trip. Do you spend all your time imagining bears mauling your tent and thunderstorms flooding your campsite, or do you focus on the excitement of building a crackling campfire, roasting marshmallows under a starlit sky, and waking up to the sound of birds singing in the trees?

Sure, it's wise to pack some rain gear and know what to do if you encounter a wild animal. But if you spend your entire trip dwelling on potential disasters, you'll miss out on all the joy and beauty that camping has to offer.

The same principle applies to life in general. Focusing on the negative will only lead to unnecessary stress and anxiety. It's like wearing a pair of sunglasses that only allow you to see the shadows, making it impossible to appreciate the vibrant colors and beauty of the world around you.

Instead, try putting on a pair of "positivity goggles" for a change. When you encounter a challenge, instead of immediately assuming the worst, see it as an opportunity for growth and learning. When you make a mistake, don't beat yourself up – instead, see it as a chance to Improve. And when you're faced with a difficult decision, focus on the potential positive outcomes instead of dwelling on the risks.

I'm not saying you should ignore reality or become blind to potential problems. But I am saying that you should choose where you focus your attention. Do you want to spend your time ruminating on what could go wrong, or do you want to focus on the possibilities and the potential for happiness?

The choice Is yours. You have the power to control your thoughts, and ultimately, your own happiness. So, what will it be? Drama Queen or Show tunes Star? The stage is yours, and the spotlight is waiting for you!

But wait, there's more! This negativity bias doesn't just haunt our personal lives – it infiltrates our relationships, careers, and even our perception of the world.

Relationship wrecker: Imagine this: you're on a date with someone you really like. You're having a good time, laughing and getting to know each other. But then, your negativity bias kicks in. You start focusing on every little thing you perceive as a flaw, from the way they chew their food to the slightly awkward joke they told. Suddenly, the spark you felt earlier starts to fade, replaced by a wave of doubt and negativity.

Career killer: You have a big presentation at work, and you've prepared for weeks. You know your material inside and out. But as you step into the conference room, your inner critic starts whispering. It tells you you're going to mess up, that everyone will laugh at you, that you're not good enough. Before you even open your mouth, your confidence is shot, and your performance suffers.

World warper: We often hear about the negativity bias in the news, where bad news gets more attention than good news. This creates a skewed perception of the world, making it seem like things are worse than they actually are. It can lead to fear, anxiety, and a sense of hopelessness.

So, what can we do to combat this negativity bias and its insidious effects? Here are a few additional strategies:

1. Practice gratitude: Take some time each day to reflect on the things you're grateful for. It could be something big, like your health or your family, or something small, like a delicious meal or a beautiful sunset. The more you focus on the good things in your life, the less power your negativity bias will have.

2. Reframe your thoughts: When you have a negative thought, try to reframe it in a more positive light. For example, instead of thinking "I'm going to fail," think "I'm going to give it my best shot, and even if I don't succeed, i'll learn something from the experience."

3. Challenge your inner critic: Don't just accept your negative thoughts as truth. Question them, challenge them, and see if they hold up under scrutiny. Often, you'll find that your inner critic is just being overly harsh and unrealistic.

4. Celebrate your successes: Take some time to celebrate your accomplishments, no matter how big or small. This will help you build confidence and positive self-esteem, making you less susceptible to negativity bias.

5. Surround yourself with positive people: Spend time with people who uplift you and make you feel good about yourself. Avoid people who are negative and critical, as they will only fuel your own negativity bias.

6. Take care of yourself: When you're stressed and tired, you're more likely to be negative. Make sure you're getting enough sleep, eating healthy foods, exercising regularly, and taking time for relaxation.

7. Seek professional help: If you're struggling to overcome your negativity bias on your own, don't be afraid to seek professional help. A therapist can teach you new coping mechanisms and help you develop a more positive outlook on life.

Remember, overcoming your negativity bias is a journey, not a destination. It takes time and effort, but it's definitely possible. By following these tips and being patient with yourself, you can learn to tame your inner Gremlin and cultivate a more positive and fulfilling life.

So go forth, brave negativity-basters! Armed with the knowledge of your brain's bizarre bias and a toolbox of positivity-boosting strategies, you are ready to conquer your inner critic, rewrite your narrative, and create a life filled with laughter, joy, and happiness. After all, the world needs more Show tunes Stars, not Drama Queens. Let your inner voice sing its positive tunes loud and proud, and watch as your life transforms into a beautiful melody of joy and fulfillment.

Chapter 2: Introducing your inner jerk:

Meet Mildred the mischief-maker

Ah, the inner voice. A constant companion, whispering doubts, anxieties, and unsolicited commentary. But let's be honest, it's rarely a wise and supportive friend. More often, it's a nagging, judgmental, and downright annoying character. So, it's time to meet the resident villain of your mind: Mildred the Mischief-Maker.

Mildred isn't your typical villain. No Darth Vader cape or world-ending plans here. Instead, she's a master of subtle sabotage, wielding negativity like a slingshot, firing tiny pebbles of doubt and insecurity at your dreams and aspirations. Imagine a cross between your grandma's gossip-loving neighbor and that troll from internet comments, but with a penchant for self-deprecating humor and a wardrobe straight out of a thrift store's "slightly used nightmares" section.

Mildred's arsenal is vast, but some of her favorite weapons include:

The never-ending comparison game: This is Mildred's classic trick. She loves pointing out all the ways you fall short compared to others, highlighting their accomplishments and successes while conveniently forgetting your own. "Look at Sarah," Mildred might whisper, "she's already published two novels, while you're still staring at a blank page."

Mildred the mischief-maker is many things, but subtle she is not. When she's not busy whispering doom and gloom forecasts or magnifying your mistakes, she's likely found her favorite weapon: the never-Ending Comparison Game.

This insidious trick is Mildred's bread and butter. It's a simple yet effective way to chip away at your self-esteem and leave you feeling discouraged and inadequate. Here's how it works:

Identify the "Perfect" Target: Mildred has an uncanny knack for finding someone to compare you to, someone who seems to have it all together. This person could be a friend, family member, colleague, or even a complete stranger you saw on social media. Whoever it is, they'll be used as the yardstick against which your own accomplishments are measured, and you'll always come up short.

Highlight their successes: Mildred has a selective memory when it comes to the achievements of others. She'll gleefully point out their promotions, awards, relationships, and seemingly perfect lives, conveniently forgetting any struggles or setbacks they might have faced. This creates an illusion of effortless success, making your own journey seem all the more difficult.

Minimize your efforts: While Mildred basks in the achievements of others, she conveniently downplays your own efforts. Your hard work, dedication, and resilience become invisible, replaced by a narrative of inadequacy and failure. "Sarah got published because she's a natural talent," Mildred might whisper, "you, on the other hand, are just a struggling writer."

Difficult self-doubt and discouragement: This is the ultimate goal of the Comparison Game. By constantly comparing yourself to others and highlighting their successes while minimizing your own, Mildred plants seeds of doubt and discouragement in your mind. You begin to question your abilities, your worth, and even your very dreams.

But fear not, fellow negativity-basters! We can outsmart Mildred's sneaky slingshot. Here are a few ways to counter the Comparison Game:

Recognize the Game: The first step to breaking free is to become aware of the game itself. When you catch yourself comparing yourself to others, acknowledge that it's Mildred's trick. Don't let her pull you into her negativity vortex.

Focus on your own journey: Instead of obsessing over someone else's path, focus on your own unique journey. Celebrate your own accomplishments, no matter how small they may seem. Every step forward, every hurdle overcome, is a victory worth acknowledging.

Embrace your uniqueness: No two people are alike. Comparing yourself to others is like comparing apples to oranges. You have your own strengths, weaknesses, and experiences that make you who you are. Embrace your individuality and stop striving for someone else's version of success.

Reframe the comparison: Instead of seeing others' success as a threat, see it as inspiration. Learn from their achievements and use them to motivate yourself. Ask yourself, "What can I learn from their journey that can help me on mine?"

Surround yourself with positivity: surround yourself with people who uplift and support you, not those who tear you down. Spend time with friends who celebrate your successes and encourage you on your journey. Avoid those who engage in constant comparisons and negativity.

Practice gratitude: Take time each day to reflect on the things you're grateful for. This includes your own unique talents, experiences, and even the challenges you've overcome. Cultivating an attitude of gratitude can help you shift your focus from what you lack to what you have.

Remember, the never-ending comparison game is just that: a game. It's a mental trap that Mildred uses to keep you feeling small and inadequate. But you don't have to play along. By recognizing the game, focusing on your own journey, and cultivating a positive mindset, you can break free from Mildred's clutches and embrace the joy and fulfillment that comes from celebrating your own unique path.

So, the next time Mildred tries to drag you into the Comparison game, remember: you are not defined by your comparison to others. You are an amazing individual with your own set of talents and strengths. Focus on your own journey, celebrate your own successes, and let your inner light shine!

The doom & gloom forecast: With Mildred around, even the sunniest day can feel like a impending storm. She loves to catastrophize every situation, predicting the worst possible outcome before anything has even happened. "Sure, you could try that new recipe," Mildred might hiss, "but you'll probably just burn it to a crisp and everyone will laugh at you."

Mildred the mischief-maker is a master manipulator, and one of her most insidious tricks is the Doom and Gloom Forecast. Armed with a magnifying glass of negativity, she scans your life for potential disasters, predicting the worst possible outcome before anything has even happened. With Mildred around, even the sunniest day can feel like a brewing storm about to unleash its fury on your dreams and aspirations.

Here's how Mildred's doom and gloom forecast works:

Identify a potential threat: Mildred has a radar for anything that deviates from your comfort zone, whether it's trying a new recipe, giving a presentation, or venturing outside your daily routine. These events become targets for her negativity, providing fertile ground for her catastrophizing tendencies.

Potentially negative thinking that can hinder the process: With laser-like focus, Mildred zooms in on every possible negative outcome. She conjures up vivid images of failure, humiliation, and disappointment, painting a dire picture of what could go wrong. She forgets to mention the potential positive outcomes, focusing solely on the dark side of the cloud.

Plant seeds of doubt and fear: armed with her arsenal of potential disasters, Mildred begins to plant seeds of doubt and fear in your mind. "Sure, you could try that new recipe," she might hiss, "but you'll probably just burn it to a crisp and everyone will laugh at you." These whispers erode your confidence and make you question your abilities, leading you to second-guess yourself and potentially avoid taking any action at all.

Keep you paralyzed by fear: The ultimate goal of Mildred's doom and gloom forecast is to keep you paralyzed by fear. She wants you to believe that the worst will inevitably happen, discouraging you from taking any risks or stepping outside your comfort zone. This can lead to missed opportunities, unfulfilled dreams, and a life lived in fear of the unknown.

But fear not, fellow positivity warriors! We can weather Mildred's stormy forecast and emerge stronger and more hopeful on the other side. Here are some tools to help you navigate the stormy seas of negativity:

Recognize the forecast: The first step to weathering the storm is to recognize it for what it is: just a forecast. It's not a guarantee, just one possible outcome amongst many. By acknowledging Mildred's negativity, you can begin to take control of your thoughts and emotions.

Challenge the catastrophizing: Don't let Mildred's predictions run wild in your mind. Challenge them with logic and reason. Ask yourself, "Is this really the most likely outcome? What are other possible scenarios?" This will help you gain a more realistic perspective and lessen the impact of her negativity.

Fopossiblyour strengths: Remember your past successes and the times you overcame challenges. Remind yourself of your skills, talents, and resilience. This will boost your confidence and help you believe in your ability to face whatever comes your way.

Visualize positive outcomes: Instead of dwelling on the negatives, visualize yourself achieving your desired outcome. Imagine yourself succeeding with your new recipe, delivering a captivating presentation, or conquering your fear of public speaking. This positive visualization will shift your focus and empower you to take action.

Surround yourself with positivity: Seek out the company of people who uplift and inspire you. Stay away from those who feed into your negativity and reinforce Mildred's gloomy forecasts. Surround yourself with sunshine and optimism, and it will be harder for Mildred's storm clouds to gather.

Practice gratitude: Take time each day to appreciate the good things in your life, both big and small. This will help you develop a more positive outlook and shift your focus away from negativity.

Remember, the doom and gloom forecast is just a storm, and it will eventually pass. By recognizing Mildred's tricks, challenging her predictions, and focusing on the positive, you can weather any storm and emerge stronger and more resilient than before. So, let the sunshine in, embrace the possibilities, and remember: the only forecast that truly matters is the one you create for yourself.

With a little bit of effort and a lot of positivity, you can turn even the most daunting forecast into a bright and sunny day. So, go out there and chase your dreams, knowing that you have the power to shape your own future, regardless of Mildred's gloomy predictions. Remember, you are the captain of your own ship, and you have the power to navigate through any storm and reach your desired destination.

The magnifying glass of mistakes: Mildred has a magnifying glass specifically for your mistakes, blowing them up to monstrous proportions while conveniently minimizing your successes. "Remember that time you tripped in front of everyone?" she'll cackle, "Everyone probably still thinks you're a clumsy fool."

The deflating balloon of confidence: Just when you start to feel good about yourself, Mildred steps in with a pin, ready to pop your bubble of confidence. "Don't get too cocky," she'll sneer, "you're bound to mess things up sooner or later."

But Mildred isn't invincible. In fact, she thrives on your attention. The more you listen to her negativity, the stronger she becomes. So, the first step to defeating her is to recognize her presence. When you hear that negative voice whispering in your ear, take a step back and acknowledge that it's Mildred, not your true self.

Next, it's time to disarm her. Don't engage in her arguments, don't try to reason with her, and don't let her guilt-trip you. Instead, laugh at her. Picture her ridiculous outfit, imagine her voice squeaking like a rusty hinge, and find the humor in her negativity. This takes away her power and reduces her to the pathetic, insecure troll that she truly is.

Finally, drown out her voice. Replace her negativity with positive affirmations, mantras, and self-compassion. Surround yourself with positive people and engage in activities that make you feel good. This will create a chorus of positivity that will drown out Mildred's squeaks and make it harder for her to be heard.

Remember, Mildred is a part of you, but she doesn't define you. You have the power to control your thoughts and choose to focus on the positive. So, don't let Mildred steal your joy. Recognize her, disarm her, and drown her out. Your life is too short to be spent listening to a troll in your head. Go out there and create a life filled with laughter, happiness, and the sweet music of your own positive thoughts.

And remember, if Mildred ever starts getting the upper hand again, just remind yourself: she may be a mischief-maker, but you are the master of your own mind. And you deserve a life filled with sunshine, not storms. So, banish the negativity, embrace the positivity, and let your inner voice sing its own melody of joy and fulfillment.

Chapter 3: The negativity hall of fame:

A guided tour of your inner jerk's museum
Welcome, fellow negativity-battlers, to the negativity hall of fame! This museum isn't your typical showcase of grandeur and beauty. Instead, it houses a collection of your inner critic's greatest hits – a menagerie of negativity in all its forms. Here, we'll explore the various flavors of your inner jerk's venom, from the self-deprecating whispers of doubt to the catastrophizing forecasts that paint your future in shades of doom and gloom.

. Exhibit A: Self-doubt, the insidious serpent

Self-doubt is the insidious serpent that slithers into our minds, coiling around our dreams and aspirations, whispering poisonous doubts and anxieties that can chip away at our confidence and leave us feeling paralyzed. It's the voice that tells us we're not good enough, not smart enough, not worthy enough. It makes us second-guess every decision, question every choice, and fear every opportunity.

Imagine self-doubt as a gremlin lurking in our shadow, a constant companion who delights in reminding us of every perceived inadequacy. It's like a broken record stuck on repeat, playing the same negative thoughts over and over again, until we start to believe them. This insidious voice can manifest in various ways:

The critic: "You're not ready for this. You'll just mess it up." This critic constantly throws up roadblocks, highlighting our perceived flaws and emphasizing the potential for failure.

The imposter: "Everyone else is so much better than you. They'll see you for the fraud you are." This imposter syndrome makes us feel like we're constantly on the verge of being exposed as incompetent, fueling our fear of success.

The catastrophizer: "This is a terrible idea. It's going to end in disaster." This voice paints a bleak picture of the future, focusing on every potential negative outcome and amplifying our anxieties to paralyzing levels.

Self-doubt isn't just an annoyance, it can have a significant impact on our lives. It can prevent us from taking risks, pursuing our dreams, and reaching our full potential. It can lead to procrastination, social isolation, and even depression.

But there's hope! We don't have to let self-doubt rule our lives. Here are some tools to combat this insidious serpent:

Recognize the voice: The first step to fighting self-doubt is to recognize it for what it is. When you hear that negative voice whispering in your ear, acknowledge it as self-doubt and challenge its legitimacy. Ask yourself, "Is this thought realistic? Is it helpful?"

Replace negative thoughts with positive affirmations: Counter the negativity of self-doubt with positive affirmations. Choose statements that resonate with you and repeat them to yourself regularly. This can help to reprogram your subconscious mind and build your confidence.

Focus on your strengths: Make a list of your strengths and accomplishments. Remind yourself of all the things you've overcome and achieved in the past. This will help you to develop a more positive self-image and increase your belief in your abilities.

Surround yourself with positivity: Spend time with people who uplift and encourage you. Avoid those who feed into your negativity and doubt. Surround yourself with positive influences who will support you on your journey to overcoming self-doubt.

Celebrate your successes: Take the time to acknowledge and celebrate your successes, no matter how small they may seem. This will help you to focus on the positive and build momentum in your life.

Seek professional help: If you find yourself struggling to overcome self-doubt on your own, don't hesitate to seek professional help. A therapist can provide valuable guidance and support as you work to silence the voice of self-doubt and embrace your full potential.

Remember, self-doubt is a common experience, but it doesn't have to define you. By recognizing its presence, challenging its negativity, and replacing it with positive self-talk and self-compassion, you can slay the insidious serpent of self-doubt and embark on a journey of self-discovery and fulfillment.

So, let not the gremlins of doubt dim your inner light. Shine brighter than their negativity, and remember, you are capable of achieving great things. Believe in yourself, embrace your strengths, and take that first step towards conquering your dreams. You are stronger than self-doubt, and you have the power to create a life filled with confidence, happiness, and success.

Exhibit B: The magnifying glass of catastrophization

Ah, the magnifying glass of catastrophization – a tool wielded by our inner jerk to distort reality and turn even the tiniest hiccup into a harbinger of doom. This warped lens zooms in on every potential negative outcome, blowing it up to monstrous proportions while conveniently shrinking our ability to see any positive possibilities.

Imagine this: you're about to give a presentation at work. Suddenly, the magnifying glass of catastrophization appears, transforming your mild nervousness into a full-blown anxiety attack. You see yourself stumbling over your words, forgetting your points, and being laughed out of the room. Your heart races, your palms sweat, and you're convinced that this presentation will be your professional demise.

This is the insidious power of catastrophization. It takes a simple event and twists it into a terrifying spectacle, robbing us of our ability to think rationally and take action. It's like a hyperactive hamster on a wheel, spinning out of control and generating worst-case scenarios faster than you can blink.

Here are some of the ways catastrophization can wreak havoc on our lives:

Paralysis by fear: When we envision every possible disaster, we can become paralyzed by fear. Taking even the smallest step forward seems too risky, and we end up avoiding opportunities and hindering our progress.

Increased anxiety and stress: The constant barrage of negative thoughts and images fuels our anxiety and stress levels. This can lead to physical and emotional health problems, making it even harder to cope with challenges.

Reduced self-esteem: When we catastrophize, we focus on all the ways we could fail or mess up. This can damage our self-esteem and make us doubt our abilities, leading to feelings of inadequacy and worthlessness.

But fear not, fellow negativity-battlers! We are not powerless against the magnifying glass of catastrophization. Here are some tools to help us reclaim control and see things in a clearer light:

Challenge negative Thoughts: When you catch yourself catastrophizing, stop and question the validity of your thoughts. Ask yourself, "Is this the most likely outcome? What are other possibilities? What evidence do I have to support this negative prediction?"

Focus on the Present Moment: Catastrophization often takes us down a rabbit hole of future possibilities, causing us to miss out on the present. Instead, try to ground yourself in the here and now. Focus on what you can control and take things one step at a time.

Practice positive visualization: Instead of focusing on the worst that could happen, visualize yourself succeeding. Imagine yourself delivering a confident presentation, overcoming challenges, and achieving your goals. This can help build your confidence and reduce anxiety.

Talk to someone you trust: sharing your worries and anxieties with a supportive friend, family member, or therapist can help you gain perspective and develop more realistic thinking patterns.

Remember your past successes: remind yourself of all the times you have faced challenges and overcome them. This will help you build resilience and trust in your ability to handle whatever comes your way.

The magnifying glass of catastrophization may be a powerful tool, but it's not an invincible one. By recognizing its effects, challenging negative thoughts, and focusing on the present moment, we can reclaim control and view our experiences through a lens of reality and possibility. Remember, the future is not set in stone, and you have the power to create a positive outcome, regardless of what your inner jerk might try to tell you. So, take a deep breath, release the magnifying glass of catastrophization, and embrace the uncertainty of life with open arms and a positive attitude.

Exhibit C: Comparisonitis, the green-eyed monster

Ah, comparisonitis, the green-eyed monster that lurks within us all. This insidious beast, disguised as innocent curiosity, slithers into our minds and plants seeds of envy and inadequacy. It compares our lives to others, magnifying their successes and minimizing their struggles, leaving us feeling like we're forever falling behind in the race of life.

Think of comparisonitis as a mischievous chameleon, constantly changing its colors to blend in with our deepest insecurities. It can morph into the seemingly perfect friend, the impeccably curated social media influencer, or even the charismatic stranger we pass on the street. Each comparison fuels the green-eyed monster within, reminding us of everything we lack and leaving us feeling incomplete and dissatisfied.

Comparisonitis operates in a number of ways, all aimed at eroding our self-esteem and happiness:

The highlight reel illusion: We compare our entire lives to the carefully curated highlights of others, often presented on social media. We see their picture-perfect vacations, their seemingly effortless achievements, and their seemingly perfect relationships. This distorted reality makes us feel like our own lives pale in comparison.

The constant competition: Comparisonitis fuels a relentless competition within us. We constantly strive to measure up to others, comparing our income, our relationships, our possessions, and even our physical appearance. This constant focus on "keeping up" can lead to feelings of inadequacy and dissatisfaction.

The devaluing of progress: Comparisonitis blinds us to our own progress. We focus on how far we have to go compared to others, ignoring the distance we've already traveled. This can demotivate us and make us feel like our efforts are meaningless.

The diminishing of joy: When we compare our lives to others, it's hard to truly appreciate the good things in our own lives. We get caught up in what we don't have, overlooking the blessings we do have. This can rob us of the joy and contentment that comes from being present and grateful.

But fear not, fellow travelers on the path to self-compassion! We can tame the green-eyed monster and break free from the shackles of comparisonitis. Here are some tools to help us on our journey:

Practice gratitude: Take time each day to reflect on the things you're grateful for, big and small. This will help you shift your focus away from what you lack and towards all the good things in your life.

Focus on your own journey: Remember that everyone has their own unique path in life. Comparing your journey to someone else's is like comparing apples to oranges. It's pointless and only leads to dissatisfaction.

Embrace your uniqueness: Each of us has our own strengths, talents, and experiences Instead of trying to be someone else, celebrate what makes you unique and special.

Surround yourself with positivity: Choose to spend time with people who uplift and inspire you. Avoid those who feed into your insecurities and engage in constant comparisons.

Be mindful of social media: Take breaks from social media and be mindful of the content you consume. Focus on accounts that inspire you and promote positivity, and avoid those that make you feel inadequate.

Celebrate others' successes: Instead of feeling envious of others' achievements, learn to celebrate them. Remember, their success doesn't diminish your own potential.

Seek professional help: If comparisonitis is taking a toll on your mental health and well-being, don't hesitate to seek professional help. A therapist can help you understand the root of your comparisonitis and develop coping mechanisms to manage it.

By recognizing the presence of comparisonitis, challenging its distorted perspectives, and cultivating a more positive and grateful outlook, we can free ourselves from the green-eyed monster's grasp. Remember, your worth is not determined by how you compare to others. You are worthy and deserving of happiness, just as you are. Embrace your individuality, celebrate your own unique journey, and let your inner light shine brightly.

Exhibit D: The perfectionism paradox: A noble pursuit gone amiss

Perfectionism, at first glance, appears noble. It's the striving for excellence, the desire to do everything flawlessly. However, beneath this seemingly virtuous facade lies a dark paradox. This unrelenting pursuit of perfection, instead of leading to success and fulfillment, often results in frustration, disappointment, and unfulfilled potential.

Imagine perfectionism as a drill sergeant, a harsh taskmaster who demands flawless execution in every endeavor. It leaves no room for error, scrutinizing every detail and condemning any perceived imperfection. This constant pressure to be perfect can be crippling. It stifles our creativity, discourages risk-taking, and prevents us from fully embracing our unique talents and abilities.

Here's how the perfectionism paradox manifests in our lives:

The tyranny of unrealistic Expectations: Perfectionism sets impossibly high standards, often exceeding what is achievable. We judge ourselves harshly for anything less than flawless, leading to a constant cycle of self-criticism and dissatisfaction.

The procrastination trap: fearing failure and the harsh judgment of our inner critic, we procrastinate on tasks, paralyzed by the fear of not being able to achieve perfection. This leads to missed opportunities and increased stress and anxiety.

The creativity killer: when we're fixated on achieving perfection, we become afraid to experiment and take risks. This stifles our creativity and prevents us from exploring new ideas and avenues.

The joy drain: the constant pursuit of perfection steals the joy from our daily activities. We become so focused on the outcome that we forget to enjoy the process itself, leading to burnout and dissatisfaction.

The comparison trap: perfectionism often leads to unhealthy comparisons with others. We measure ourselves against others' perceived perfection, failing to recognize their own struggles and the uniqueness of our own journeys.

However, there's hope! We can break free from the shackles of perfectionism and embrace a more balanced and fulfilling approach. Here are some tools to help you on this journey:

Redefine success: shift your focus from achieving perfection to striving for progress and growth. Celebrate your efforts and milestones, regardless of whether they are flawless or not.

embrace imperfections: accept that mistakes and imperfections are a natural part of life and learning. View them as opportunities to learn and grow, not as failures to be condemned.

Practice self-compassion: be kind and understanding to yourself. Forgive yourself for your mistakes and focus on learning from them.

Focus on your strengths: celebrate your strengths and talents. Recognize that everyone has unique abilities and that you don't need to be perfect in everything to be worthy.

Set realistic goals: set realistic and achievable goals that focus on progress rather than perfection. Break down large tasks into smaller, more manageable steps.

celebrate the journey: enjoy the process of learning, creating, and growing. Don't be so fixated on the outcome that you miss out on the joy of the journey itself.

Seek support: surround yourself with supportive people who encourage you to embrace your imperfections and celebrate your progress. Consider seeking professional help if you find yourself struggling to overcome perfectionism on your own.

Remember, perfectionism is an illusion. It's a pursuit that can never be fully attained and ultimately leads to frustration and despair. By embracing a more balanced approach, focusing on progress and self-acceptance, we can break free from the perfectionism paradox and unlock our true potential. Allow yourself to make mistakes, embrace your imperfections, and enjoy the journey of life, for it is in the imperfections that we discover our true beauty and strength.

The procrastination pitfall: where comfort turns into regret

Ah, procrastination, the seductive armchair that beckons us with promises of comfort and relaxation. It whispers sweet nothings about needing "just a little more time" before we need to face our responsibilities. But nestled within this seemingly harmless comfort lies a cunning foe, one that can lull us into a state of complacency and ultimately trap us in its clutches.

Procrastination is the master of avoidance, expertly masking itself as a harmless indulgence. It encourages us to bury our heads in the sand, to postpone dealing with difficult or unpleasant situations, and to prioritize immediate gratification over long-term goals. It's the voice that whispers, "just five more minutes," as you scroll through endless social media feeds, or the rationalization that convinces you to start that important project "tomorrow" instead of today.

Imagine procrastination as a living entity, a mischievous gremlin that delights in seeing us flounder. It sits comfortably in your subconscious, patiently waiting for the moment you need to focus and take action. Then, in a flash, it transforms your to-do list into a daunting mountain, amplifying your anxieties and making even the smallest task seem insurmountable.

This insidious gremlin operates in various ways, each contributing to a cycle of procrastination and regret:

The illusion of control: Procrastination offers a false sense of control. We believe that by putting things off, we somehow regain control over our time and responsibilities. However, this illusion quickly fades as deadlines loom and the pressure mounts, leaving us feeling overwhelmed and powerless.

The fear of failure: Underlying procrastination often lies a deep fear of failure. We avoid tasks because we're afraid of not being good enough, of not meeting our own expectations or those of others. This fear can be paralyzing, preventing us from even attempting to start, let alone finish, a task.

The lure of instant gratification: procrastination thrives on short-term pleasure. It offers the immediate satisfaction of checking out of our responsibilities and indulging in distractions, making it difficult to resist the allure of the moment and prioritize long-term goals.

The perfectionist trap: procrastination can be a symptom of perfectionism. We set impossibly high standards for ourselves, believing that anything less than flawless is unacceptable. This fear of not achieving perfection leads us to procrastinate, hoping that somehow, with more time, we'll be able to magically produce something perfect.

The cycle of anxiety and regret: procrastination fuels a vicious cycle of anxiety and regret. As deadlines approach and tasks remain incomplete, our anxiety levels rise, leading us to engage in further avoidance and procrastination. This cycle can leave us feeling demoralized, unproductive, and ultimately filled with regret for not taking action sooner.

But fear not! We are not powerless against the insidious gremlin of procrastination. By recognizing its tactics, understanding its triggers, and equipping ourselves with the right tools, we can escape its clutches and reclaim control over our time and goals. Here are some tools to help you conquer procrastination:

Identify your triggers: what are the situations, emotions, or tasks that typically lead you to procrastinate? Recognizing these triggers allows you to anticipate them and develop strategies to resist their pull.

Set realistic goals: break down large tasks into smaller, more manageable steps. This makes them less overwhelming and reduces the feeling of being stuck.

Prioritize your tasks: determine which tasks are most important and urgent, and focus on completing them first. This helps ensure that you're making progress and not neglecting crucial responsibilities.

Create a routine: establish a regular schedule for working on specific tasks. This helps to build accountability and consistency, making it easier to avoid procrastination.

Reward yourself: celebrate your accomplishments, no matter how small. This helps to stay motivated and reinforces the positive behavior of taking action.

Find a support system: surround yourself with people who encourage and support your goals. Sharing your struggles and seeking advice can be a valuable tool in overcoming procrastination.

Practice mindfulness: when you find yourself procrastinating, take a step back and observe your thoughts and emotions without judgment. This allows you to gain a clearer perspective and make conscious choices about how to move forward.

Remember, procrastination is a common human experience. By understanding its nature and applying these strategies, you can break free from its clutches and embrace a more productive and fulfilling life. So, turn off the netflix, silence the notifications, and step away from the comfort of the procrastination armchair. Take that first step, embrace the discomfort, and embark on a journey of accomplishment and self-discovery.

Exhibit f: the negativity feedback loop: a downward spiral

Ah, the negativity feedback loop – a self-fulfilling prophecy of sorts, weaving a web of pessimism and despair. It begins with a single, seemingly insignificant negative thought, a whisper in the back of your mind. This thought, like a seed, takes root and grows, nurtured by negativity's fertile soil.

Fueled by this initial negativity, emotions begin to cloud your judgment. Optimism wanes, replaced by feelings of frustration, disappointment, and even anger. These emotions act as amplifiers, magnifying the negativity and drawing your focus further into the darkness.

This is where the loop begins to spin. The negative thoughts, now intensified by their emotional counterparts, trigger yet another wave of negativity. Your mind becomes a breeding ground for pessimism, churning out self-doubt, self-criticism, and a sense of hopelessness.

Like a hamster on a wheel, you find yourself running in circles, unable to escape the negativity's pull. It feels as though you're trapped in a dark abyss, surrounded by walls of pessimism and despair. The outside world, once full of possibilities, fades into a distant echo, replaced by the deafening din of negativity in your mind.

negativity feedback loop, while powerful, is not invincible. There are tools and strategies that can help you break free from its grip and step into the light.

1. Recognize the cycle: the first step to breaking free is to become aware of the loop's presence. Pay attention to your thoughts and emotions, identifying triggers that lead you down the path of negativity.

2. Challenge negative thoughts: don't accept negative thoughts as absolute truths. Question their validity and seek evidence to counter them. Look for alternative perspectives and remind yourself of your strengths and accomplishments.

3. Reframe your focus: instead of dwelling on the negative, actively shift your focus to the positive aspects of your life. Practice gratitude for the good things you have, no matter how small they may seem.

4. Surround yourself with positivity: seek out positive and supportive people who uplift your spirits and encourage you. Limit your exposure to negativity and toxic relationships.

5. Engage in activities you enjoy: make time for activities that bring you joy and fulfillment. Engaging in hobbies, spending time in nature, or practicing mindfulness can help to counteract negativity and cultivate a sense of peace and well-being.

6. Seek professional help: if you find yourself struggling to break free from the negativity feedback loop on your own, don't hesitate to seek professional help. A therapist can provide valuable guidance and support as you develop healthier coping mechanisms and reclaim control over your thoughts and emotions.

Remember, the negativity feedback loop is not a permanent state of being. It may seem powerful, but it is not your destiny. By recognizing its presence, challenging negative thoughts, and actively seeking positivity, you can break free from its grip and step into a brighter, more fulfilling future. Choose hope over despair, optimism over pessimism, and remember – you have the power to change your story.

But fear not, negativity-battlers! The exhibits in this hall may not be pleasant, but understanding the different flavors of negativity is the first step to conquering them. By recognizing these negative thought patterns and their effects, you can begin to challenge them and replace them with more positive and empowering thoughts.

Remember, you are not powerless over your inner critic. You have the power to choose your thoughts and refuse to be ruled by negativity. With awareness, self-compassion, and the right tools, you can transform your negativity.

Part 2: tools to evict your inner jerk (and replace him with a cheer squad)

Chapter 4: the gratitude gremlin

Deep within the labyrinthine caverns of the human mind, where shadows dance and anxieties whisper, dwells a creature unlike any other. This adorable, mischievous being, known as the gratitude gremlin, thrives on disrupting negativity spirals with random bursts of appreciation.

Imagine a tiny gremlin, no bigger than your thumb, with bright, curious eyes and a mischievous grin. Its fur shimmers with a kaleidoscope of colors, reflecting the multitude of positive emotions it embodies. Unlike its monstrous cousins who breed fear and doubt, the gratitude gremlin is a beacon of hope and joy, flitting through the mental landscape, scattering seeds of gratitude in its wake.

But don't let its size fool you. The gratitude gremlin is a master of the unexpected. It chooses its moments with calculated precision, intervening just as your mind begins to sink into the quicksand of negativity. A single negative thought, a fleeting moment of self-doubt, and suddenly, the gremlin appears, perched on your shoulder, its tiny head tilted in amusement.

With a mischievous glint in its eyes, the gremlin performs a curious ritual. It claps its tiny hands, generating a ripple of positive energy that washes over your consciousness. As the wave of negativity recedes, the gremlin starts whispering, not words, but emotions. It transmits feelings of gratitude, appreciation, and joy, reorienting your focus towards the blessings in your life.

The gremlin might remind you of that warm hug from a loved one, the breathtaking beauty of a sunrise, the simple joy of a delicious meal. It might even highlight the resilience you've shown during past challenges or the progress you've made towards your goals. Each reminder, no matter how small, acts as a counter-spell, breaking the negative thought patterns and replacing them with a sense of thankfulness.

But the gremlin's magic isn't limited to mere interruption. It possesses an uncanny ability to shift your perspective. Suddenly, challenges become opportunities for growth, failures become stepping stones to success, and setbacks become lessons to learn from. The gremlin helps you see the silver lining, the hidden blessings, and the beauty within the storm.

This shift in perspective is transformative. It allows you to appreciate the present moment, to find joy in the everyday, and to cultivate a sense of optimism about the future. With each burst of gratitude, the gremlin helps you build an inner reservoir of resilience and strength, making you less susceptible to negativity's pull.

However, the gremlin's work isn't without its challenges. It faces fierce opposition from its monstrous cousins – the Doubt Gremlin, the Fear Gremlin, and the Self-Criticism Gremlin. These negativity-fueled creatures are constantly on the lookout, eager to undo the gremlin's good work and drag you back into the darkness.

But the gratitude gremlin is not easily discouraged. It knows the power of its magic, the transformative potential of gratitude. It continues to flit through your mind, leaving behind its tiny seeds of appreciation, waiting for them to bloom into a garden of positivity.

The more you cultivate gratitude in your life, the stronger the gremlin becomes. Its visits become more frequent, its bursts of joy more potent. You learn to anticipate its arrival, to recognize the signs of its presence, and to welcome its transformative magic.

The gratitude gremlin is a reminder that despite the darkness within, there is always room for light. It teaches us to see the good, to find joy in the small things, and to appreciate the blessings in our lives. In its playful, mischievous way, the gremlin helps us cultivate a positive outlook, build resilience, and unlock the wellspring of joy that lies within us all.

So, the next time you find yourself sinking into negativity, take a moment to listen. You might just hear the tiny clap of the gratitude gremlin's hands, a signal that hope and joy are still within reach. Embrace its magic, cultivate its presence, and let the gremlin guide you towards a brighter, more grateful life.

the gratitude gremlin's playbook: cultivating joy in everyday life

The gratitude gremlin is more than just a whimsical creature. It embodies a powerful philosophy, a way of life that prioritizes joy and appreciation. But how can we, mere mortals, tap into this gremlin's wisdom and cultivate gratitude in our own lives?

The gremlin's playbook offers a collection of practices, each designed to awaken the dormant gratitude within us.

. Unveiling the hidden wonders: the power of observation

In our hurried lives, we often rush through our days, eyes glazed over, oblivious to the beauty that surrounds us. We miss the intricate details, the small wonders that paint our world with vibrant colors and whisper tales of joy. This is where the mischievous gratitude gremlin steps in, nudging us to become keen observers, to open our eyes and hearts to the magic hidden in plain sight.

The gremlin encourages us to slow down, to break free from the autopilot mode of daily life and truly see the world around us. It invites us to engage with our senses, to feel the warmth of the sun on our skin, the coolness of the breeze against our face, the gentle caress of a petal on our fingertips. It asks us to listen to the symphony of nature - the chirping of birds, the rustling of leaves, the soothing murmur of a stream. By fully immersing ourselves in the sensory experience, we awaken a sense of awe and wonder that enriches our lives.

But the gremlin's message goes beyond mere sensory indulgence. It encourages us to become detectives of the ordinary, to observe the intricate details that most people overlook. We are invited to examine the delicate veins of a leaf, the mesmerizing patterns on a butterfly's wings, the unique texture of a stone. By focusing on these seemingly insignificant things, we discover a hidden world of beauty, a testament to the artistry woven into the fabric of our existence.

The gremlin also reminds us to appreciate the ephemeral nature of beauty. It encourages us to cherish the fleeting joy of a child's laughter, the breathtaking spectacle of a sunset, the delicate lifespan of a flower. By recognizing the transience of these moments, we learn to appreciate them even more, savoring their precious presence before they fade away.

Furthermore, the gremlin guides us to connect with nature, to immerse ourselves in the awe-inspiring beauty of the natural world. Whether it's a hike through the mountains, a walk in the forest, or simply sitting quietly in our backyard, observing the interconnectedness of all living things fosters a sense of belonging and oneness with the universe.

The power of observation is not merely a passive exercise; it's a transformative practice. By consciously noticing the small things, we cultivate a deeper appreciation for the blessings in our lives. Our focus shifts from negativity to gratitude, from anxiety to hope. We become more mindful of the present moment, savoring each experience with a newfound sense of wonder.

So, open your eyes, awaken your senses, and embrace the power of observation. Let the gratitude gremlin be your guide on this journey of discovery. As you unveil the hidden wonders of the world, you will unlock a treasure chest of joy, peace, and gratitude, enriching your life in ways you never imagined.

The gratitude journal: a sanctuary for joy and appreciation

The mischievous gratitude gremlin, with its glint of mischief and boundless enthusiasm, champions a simple yet powerful practice - the gratitude journal.

This unassuming tool, a dedicated space to capture and cherish our blessings, holds the key to unlocking the hidden treasure of joy and appreciation within each of us.

Imagine a book, its pages waiting patiently to be filled with stories of gratitude. The gremlin urges us to write down everything and anything we are grateful for, big or small. Did a delicious cup of coffee brighten your morning? Jot it down! Did a friend's kind gesture fill your heart with warmth? Capture it on paper! Did a breathtaking sunset leave you speechless with wonder? Give it a place in your journal!

By faithfully recording these moments, we shift our attention away from negativity, the ever-present shadow lurking in our minds. The focus shifts from anxieties and worries to the abundance of blessings that color our lives. As we write, a sense of gratitude washes over us, washing away negativity and replacing it with a newfound appreciation for all that is good in our world.

But the magic of the gratitude journal extends beyond the moment of writing. As we revisit our entries over time, they serve as a powerful reminder of the blessings we often take for granted. We rediscover the joy of a simple act of kindness, the warmth of a loved one's presence, the beauty of a fleeting moment captured in time. Each entry becomes a testament to the richness of our lives, a gentle nudge reminding us of the good that surrounds us, even when darkness threatens to engulf us.

The gratitude journal is more than just a collection of words; it's a sanctuary for joy and appreciation. It's a safe space to express our deepest gratitude, free from judgment and self-criticism. It's a mirror reflecting the abundance of blessings that are often hidden in plain sight. As we cultivate this practice, we create a reservoir of positivity within ourselves, a wellspring from which we can draw strength and hope whenever we need it most.

So, embrace the wisdom of the gratitude gremlin. Start your own gratitude journal today. Let it become your confidante, your companion on the journey of cultivating joy and appreciation. As you fill its pages with the stories of your blessings, you will discover a world overflowing with beauty, love, and the magic of gratitude.

The thank-you ritual: the gremlin believes in the transformative power of expressing gratitude. It encourages us to incorporate a thank-you ritual into our daily lives. This could involve writing a heartfelt letter expressing gratitude to a loved one, expressing thanks for a delicious meal, or simply taking a moment to silently acknowledge the blessings we have. By consciously expressing gratitude, we amplify its positive effects and cultivate a deeper sense of appreciation.

the random acts of kindness: The gremlin reminds us that gratitude is not a passive emotion. It encourages us to actively express our appreciation through random acts of kindness. This could involve helping a stranger, offering a compliment, or simply doing something thoughtful for someone close to us. These acts of kindness not only benefit the recipient but also strengthen our own sense of joy and connection with others.

The mindfulness practice: The gremlin advocates for the practice of mindfulness. By being present in the moment and observing our thoughts and emotions without judgment, we gain a deeper understanding of ourselves and our experiences. This mindful awareness helps us appreciate the simple joys of everyday life, from the warmth of the sun on our skin to the company of loved ones.

The reframing challenge: The gremlin teaches us the art of reframing. It encourages us to challenge negative thoughts and perspectives and replace them with gratitude. Instead of focusing on what we lack, we can choose to appreciate what we have. When faced with a challenge, we can see it as an opportunity for growth and learning. By reframing our perspective, we shift our focus from negativity to gratitude, opening ourselves up to a more fulfilling and positive experience.

The celebration of imperfection: The gremlin dispels the myth of perfection. It reminds us that beauty and joy can be found in the midst of imperfection. We can learn to appreciate our quirks, imperfections, and vulnerabilities as part of what makes us unique and special. By embracing our imperfections, we release the pressure to be perfect and allow ourselves to experience genuine joy and happiness.

The gratitude gremlin's playbook is not a rigid set of rules but rather a collection of guiding principles. As we incorporate these practices into our lives, we cultivate a deeper sense of gratitude, not just for the big things but also for the small joys that make up our everyday experiences.

Remember, gratitude is a journey, not a destination. It requires ongoing practice and effort. But the rewards are immeasurable. By embracing the gremlin's wisdom, we unlock a world of joy, peace, and fulfillment, transforming our lives into a vibrant tapestry of gratitude and appreciation.

So, open your heart to the Gratitude Gremlin's message. Let it guide you towards a life filled with joy, appreciation, and the magic of seeing the good in every situation. Remember, even the smallest seed of gratitude, nurtured with care and attention, can blossom into a beautiful garden of happiness and fulfillment.

Chapter 5: Reverse mantras

Flip your limiting beliefs on their head

Have you ever noticed how easily negative self-talk can become ingrained in your brain? We carry around these self-deprecating mantras like heavy burdens, constantly reminding ourselves of our limitations and weaknesses. "I'm not good enough," "I'm not smart enough," "i'll never succeed" - these whispers in the back of our minds can become paralyzing.

But what if we could turn these negative narratives on their heads? What if we could use humor and absurdity to disarm our self-doubt and rewrite our inner scripts? This is the power of reverse mantras.

Reverse mantras are affirmations that take our deepest fears and insecurities and turn them into ridiculously exaggerated statements. Instead of reinforcing negativity, they use humor to expose the absurdity of our self-imposed limitations. By saying the opposite of what we truly believe, we can create a sense of cognitive dissonance and start to question the validity of our negative self-talk.

Imagine instead of saying, "I'm terrible at public speaking," you say, "I am incapable of remembering anything important! My mind will go blank, my voice will crack, and everyone will be staring at me in judgment." Sounds pretty ridiculous, doesn't it? By exaggerating your fear to the point of absurdity, you begin to see it for what it really is - an unhelpful and irrational thought pattern.

Here are some examples of reverse mantras:

Instead of: "I'm not creative." Try: "My brain is a barren wasteland of unoriginality. My attempt at art will be so atrocious it will induce vomiting in anyone who dares to look at it."

Instead of: "I'm afraid of heights." Try: "I am a gravity magnet! The Earth's pull on me is so strong that I will spontaneously launch myself off any ledge within a ten-foot radius."

Instead of: "I'm always late." Try: "Time is a mere suggestion to me. I adhere to my own personal time vortex, where deadlines are irrelevant and punctuality is a disease."

Instead of: "I'm not good at socializing." Try: "My social skills are so abysmal that my presence will clear a room faster than a fire alarm. Awkward silences and uncomfortable stares are my signature party tricks."

Instead of: "I'm afraid of failure." Try: "Success is my kryptonite. The mere thought of achieving anything meaningful will send me into a paralyzing spiral of self-doubt and procrastination."

It's important to approach reverse mantras with a sense of humor and playfulness. Don't take them too seriously, as the goal is not to reinforce negativity, but to deconstruct it. By laughing at our own self-doubt, we can start to loosen its hold on our minds and create space for more positive and empowering beliefs.

Here are some tips for using reverse mantras effectively:

Start small: Choose a negative belief that feels relatively minor. The more ridiculous you make your statement, the more effective it will be.

Practice regularly: Repeat your reverse mantra throughout the day, especially when you start to feel the negative thoughts creep in.

Combine with positive affirmations: Once you've disrupted the negative thought pattern with humor, follow it up with a positive affirmation that reinforces the opposite quality.

Be patient: Changing ingrained thought patterns takes time and effort. Be patient with yourself and keep practicing your reverse mantras.

Remember, reverse mantras are not a magic cure-all. They are a powerful tool that can be used to challenge limiting beliefs and open the door to self-acceptance and positive change. So, take a deep breath, embrace the absurdity, and flip your limiting beliefs on their head. You might just surprise yourself at what you're capable of achieving.

Beyond the laughter: exploring the deeper benefits of reverse mantras

While the comedic aspect of reverse mantras is readily apparent, their benefits extend far beyond mere amusement. Beneath the surface of absurdity lies a potent tool for self-discovery and personal growth. Let's delve deeper into the transformative potential of this unique practice.

Challenging the inner critic:

The inner critic, that relentless voice whispering doubt and fear, is a common foe we all face. It feeds on negativity and thrives on reminding us of our perceived shortcomings. But reverse mantras offer a powerful tool to challenge and disarm this inner saboteur.

By exaggerating our insecurities to the point of absurdity, we can expose the illogicality of our fears and challenge the inner critic's authority. Through humor, we create a distance from the negativity, recognizing it for what it is: unhelpful and untrue.

This playful approach shifts the power dynamics, allowing us to rewrite the negative scripts that often play in our heads. By taking control of the narrative, we become the antagonist of our inner critic, refusing to let it define us.

Increased self-awareness is a key benefit of using reverse mantras. By recognizing our self-deprecating thoughts, we can begin to challenge and replace them with positive affirmations. This understanding allows us to acknowledge our limitations without letting them become our identity.

As we laugh at our own fears and insecurities, a sense of self-acceptance emerges. We learn that everyone experiences self-doubt and imperfections, freeing us from the pressure of achieving an unattainable ideal. This acceptance fosters compassion and understanding for ourselves, allowing us to embrace our unique strengths and weaknesses.

The cycle of negativity is often difficult to break, but reverse mantras offer a powerful intervention. Humor injects a dose of absurdity that interrupts the flow of negativity, creating space for positive thoughts and self-affirmations to take root.

Ultimately, challenging the inner critic with reverse mantras leads to a more authentic life. We embrace our imperfections and true selves, expressing our talents and pursuing our passions without fear of judgment or self-doubt. This journey leads to greater joy, fulfillment, and purpose in life.

Remember, the key to challenging your inner critic with reverse mantras is a playful spirit and a willingness to experiment. So, unleash your inner comedian, laugh at your fears, and explore the transformative power of self-compassion and humor.

Cultivating self-compassion:

Self-compassion, the ability to treat ourselves with kindness and understanding, is often difficult to achieve. However, reverse mantras offer a unique and powerful tool to cultivate this essential quality.

By exaggerating our flaws to a humorous degree, we create a distance from our perceived shortcomings. This allows us to see them with greater objectivity and humor, recognizing them as common human experiences rather than personal failings. This shift in perspective opens the door to accepting ourselves with all our imperfections, fostering self-love and understanding.

Reverse mantras cultivate self-compassion through several key ways:

Normalizing imperfection: When we laugh at our own anxieties and insecurities, we normalize the human experience. We recognize that everyone struggles with self-doubt and limitations, and that we are not alone in our challenges. This realization removes the shame and stigma often associated with imperfection, allowing us to accept ourselves with greater ease.

Reducing self-judgment: The exaggerated nature of reverse mantras disrupts the cycle of self-criticism. When we focus on the absurdity of our self-deprecating thoughts, we lose our grip on their negativity. This allows us to loosen the hold of self-judgment and approach ourselves with greater kindness and understanding.

Fostering empathy: The act of laughing at ourselves can surprisingly lead to increased empathy for others. When we recognize our own shared humanity, it becomes easier to connect with and understand the struggles of others. This increased empathy promotes compassion and creates a more positive and supportive environment for everyone.

Building resilience: accepting our imperfections with humor allows us to develop greater resilience in the face of challenges and setbacks. When we anticipate and even exaggerate potential failures, they become less intimidating and lose their power to hold us back. This allows us to bounce back from adversity with greater ease and a sense of humor, maintaining our optimism and confidence.

Releasing control: Striving for perfection can be a source of immense stress and anxiety. Reverse mantras encourage us to release our grip on control and embrace the inherent uncertainty of life. By acknowledging and even celebrating our perceived flaws, we let go of the pressure to be perfect, allowing ourselves to be more present and authentic in the moment.

Enjoying the journey: When we focus on the humor and absurdity of our lives, we open ourselves to a greater sense of joy and appreciation. We learn to find amusement in our everyday experiences, even the challenging ones. This playful approach to life allows us to savor the journey and find happiness in the simple things.

By incorporating reverse mantras into your daily life, you can begin to cultivate a more compassionate and accepting relationship with yourself. Remember, self-compassion is not about ignoring your flaws, but about recognizing and accepting them with kindness and understanding. As you embrace your imperfections with humor, you pave the way for a more fulfilling and joyful life.

Chapter 6 Building resilience:

How reverse mantras help us bounce back:

Anticipating failure: By exaggerating potential failures through reverse mantras, we take away their power to surprise us. When we anticipate the worst-case scenario, even in a humorous way, it becomes less intimidating and we are less likely to be thrown off track by setbacks.

Developing a thicker skin: Reverse mantras help us develop a thicker skin by desensitizing us to criticism and negative feedback. When we laugh at our own self-deprecating statements, we become less affected by the negativity directed towards us by others.

Embracing humor: Humor is a powerful tool for coping with stress and adversity. By injecting humor into our self-talk, we can maintain a positive outlook even in difficult situations. This allows us to bounce back from setbacks with greater ease and resilience.

Shifting perspective: Reverse mantras encourage us to shift our perspective on failure. Instead of seeing it as a defeat, we can view it as a learning opportunity. This change in perspective allows us to approach challenges with a sense of curiosity and openness, rather than fear and anxiety.

Developing grit: Resilience is not about never experiencing setbacks, but about having the grit and determination to keep going despite them. Reverse mantras can help us develop this grit by fostering a sense of humor and optimism, even in the face of adversity.

Here are some examples of reverse mantras for building resilience:

"I am a failure magnet! Setbacks are like moths to a flame, they are drawn to me irresistibly."

"My confidence is a fragile butterfly that will shatter with the slightest criticism."

"I am a walking disaster zone, waiting to happen. Expect the worst from me always."

"I am allergic to success. If I get too close to achieving a goal, I will break out in hives of anxiety."

"Challenges are my kryptonite. They render me weak and helpless, like a deflated balloon."

It is important to remember that the key to using reverse mantras effectively is to approach them with a playful and lighthearted attitude. Don't take them too seriously, and don't use them as a way to beat yourself up. Instead, see them as a tool for self-awareness and empowerment.

By incorporating reverse mantras into your daily life, you can develop greater resilience and bounce back from life's challenges with humor, grace, and determination. Remember, the journey to success is rarely smooth, and setbacks are inevitable. But by embracing humor and self-compassion, we can turn these setbacks into stepping stones on our path to achieving our goals.

Unlocking creativity

Humor and absurdity, often seen as frivolous pursuits, hold a hidden power: the power to unlock creativity. By playfully exaggerating our limitations, we open ourselves to new perspectives, ignite the spark of innovation, and break free from the stifling grip of self-doubt.

Think of a child at play. Unburdened by self-consciousness and societal expectations, they approach the world with a wonder and endless possibility. They readily embrace the absurd, turning cardboard boxes into spaceships and transforming everyday objects into fantastical creatures. This unrestrained creativity is a testament to the inherent power of play and humor.

As adults, we often lose sight of this playful spirit. We become bogged down by self-doubt, fearing failure and ridicule. This fear can act as a barrier to creativity, preventing us from exploring new ideas and venturing outside our comfort zones.

This is where reverse mantras come in. By exaggerating our limitations to the point of absurdity, we inject humor into our self-talk, undermining the authority of our inner critic. This allows us to view our perceived shortcomings in a new light, recognizing them as potential springboards for creativity rather than insurmountable obstacles.

Reverse mantras unlock creativity in several ways:

Disrupting negative thought patterns: Negative self-talk can cripple creativity. By injecting humor into our inner dialogue, we disrupt these negative patterns and create space for new ideas to flourish.

Embracing the unexpected: When we exaggerate our limitations, we open ourselves to unexpected possibilities. We begin to see the world in a new light, recognizing potential for innovation in the most ordinary things.

Experimentation without Fear: Humor encourages us to experiment without fear of failure. When we embrace the absurd, we are less afraid to take risks and explore unconventional approaches. This can lead to breakthroughs and discoveries that would have been impossible if we remained shackled by fear of failure.

Breaking down barriers: Reverse mantras can help us break down the mental barriers that often limit our creativity. By exaggerating our perceived shortcomings, we expose their absurdity and challenge their authority. This allows us to see beyond our limitations and envision new possibilities.

Fostering collaboration: Humor can be a powerful tool for building rapport and fostering collaboration. When we laugh together at our shared anxieties and insecurities, it creates a space of trust and understanding, which is essential for creative collaboration.

Discovering hidden talents: We often underestimate our own potential. Reverse mantras can help us discover hidden talents and abilities that we never knew we possessed. By pushing ourselves outside our comfort zones and embracing the absurd, we unlock new avenues for self-expression and creativity.

Maintaining a playful spirit: as we age, we often lose touch with our inner child, the playful spirit that fueled our creativity in youth. Reverse mantras help us reconnect with this playful spirit, allowing us to approach life with a sense of humor and wonder. This playful attitude is essential for fostering creativity and innovation.

By incorporating reverse mantras into your daily life, you can tap into a powerful source of creativity and unlock your own unique potential. So, embrace the absurd, laugh at your limitations, and watch as your creativity takes flight! Remember, the most innovative ideas often come from the most unexpected places, and sometimes, all it takes is a little humor to unlock them.

5.Boosting confidence:

Boosting confidence: Finding strength in our flaws

In our world obsessed with perfection, striving for confidence can feel overwhelming. Bombarded with messages about what we "should" be, we succumb to self-doubt and insecurity. But what if the key to boosting our confidence lies not in achieving an unattainable ideal, but in embracing our imperfections instead?

Reverse mantras offer a powerful tool for this shift. By exaggerating our perceived flaws to absurdity, we inject humor into our self-talk. This playful approach disarms our inner critic and helps us view limitations not as obstacles, but as unique characteristics that contribute to who we are. This newfound self-acceptance becomes the foundation for greater confidence and self-assuredness.

Here's how embracing imperfection through reverse mantras can boost your confidence:

Redefining perfection: The pursuit of unrealistic perfection fuels self-doubt. Reverse mantras help us redefine perfection for ourselves. We come to understand that imperfections are not flaws, but simply part of being human. This shift allows us to accept ourselves as we are, quirks and limitations included.

Disarming the Inner Critic: Our inner critic thrives on negativity and self-doubt. By exaggerating our limitations with humor, we take away its power. We turn its negativity into something playful and absurd, making it easier to dismiss its harmful messages.

Embracing authenticity: When we embrace our imperfections, we become more authentic versions of ourselves. We shed the masks we wear to conform and allow our true selves to shine through. This authenticity is a source of inner strength and confidence, allowing us to connect with others on a deeper level.

Building self-compassion: Laughter and humor foster self-compassion. When we laugh at ourselves, we show ourselves kindness and understanding. This allows us to be more forgiving of our mistakes and shortcomings, leading to greater self-acceptance and confidence.

Reducing Fear of Failure: The fear of failure often hinders us from achieving our goals and fulfilling our potential. By exaggerating the possibility of failure through reverse mantras, we desensitize ourselves to its threat. This allows us to approach challenges with courage and a willingness to take risks, ultimately boosting our confidence.

Embracing risks and challenges: Stepping outside our comfort zones is essential for growth and development. Reverse mantras encourage us to embrace risks and challenges by highlighting the absurdity of our self-doubt.

This playful approach allows us to explore new possibilities and overcome our fears, leading to increased confidence and self-belief.

Reframing Mistakes as Learning Opportunities: When we see our mistakes as learning opportunities rather than failures, we can use them to grow and develop. Reverse mantras help us reframe our mistakes in this positive light by magnifying their potential for learning and growth. This shift fosters a growth mindset, boosting our confidence and resilience.

Accepting Change and Growth: Life is a constant process of change and growth. By embracing our imperfections, we open ourselves to this possibility. We recognize that our limitations are not fixed, but can be transformed and overcome. This acceptance fosters a sense of empowerment and confidence, allowing us to embrace the journey of life with greater joy and optimism.

By incorporating reverse mantras into your daily life, you can embark on a journey of self-discovery and acceptance. You can learn to embrace your imperfections, disarm your inner critic, and step into your authentic self. This newfound self-acceptance lies at the heart of true confidence, empowering you to face the world with courage, strength, and a playful spirit. Remember, your imperfections are not weaknesses, but unique characteristics that make you who you are. Embrace them, celebrate them, and watch your confidence soar.

6.Strengthening relationships:.

Strengthening relationships: The power of shared laughter and vulnerability

In a world increasingly dominated by carefully curated online personas and facades of perfection, genuine connection and heartfelt engagement can seem elusive. We often strive to project an image of flawlessness, masking our anxieties and insecurities behind a veneer of self-assuredness. But what if the key to forging deeper relationships lies not in concealing our imperfections, but in embracing them and sharing them with others?

This is where the practice of reverse mantras takes center stage. By exaggerating our perceived flaws to the point of absurdity, we inject humor into our self-talk and create a space for vulnerability and authenticity. This playful approach allows us to disarm both our own inner critic and the potential judgment of others. It invites them to see us not as flawless beings, but as human individuals with quirks and insecurities, just like them.

Sharing our reverse mantras with others can serve as a powerful catalyst for strengthening relationships in several ways:

Building Bridges through Shared Laughter: Laughter is a universal language that transcends cultural and social barriers. When we laugh together at our shared anxieties and insecurities, it creates a sense of camaraderie and reminds us that we're not alone in our struggles. This shared experience fosters connection and understanding, laying the groundwork for deeper bonds.

Enhancing empathy and compassion: By revealing our vulnerabilities and imperfections, we encourage others to do the same. This openness creates a safe space for mutual understanding and empathy. We begin to see each other not as idealized figures, but as fellow travelers on the journey of life, navigating the same challenges and uncertainties. This fosters compassion and strengthens the bonds of friendship.

Encouraging authenticity and transparency: In a world obsessed with appearances, the courage to be vulnerable and authentic is a rare and precious quality. Sharing our reverse mantras demonstrates a willingness to be open and genuine, setting the stage for others to do the same. This mutual transparency fosters authentic connection and strengthens relationships built upon trust and vulnerability.

Promoting self-acceptance and confidence: When we see others embracing their flaws and imperfections with humor and self-compassion, it inspires us to do the same. Witnessing others laugh at their own quirks and limitations encourages us to accept ourselves with all our imperfections. This self-acceptance becomes the foundation for greater confidence and self-esteem, ultimately strengthening our relationships with others.

Breaking down walls and fostering connection: Our anxieties and insecurities often act as invisible walls that separate us from others. By sharing our reverse mantras, we break down these walls and create opportunities for genuine connection. This vulnerability opens the door for deeper conversations and fosters a sense of trust and intimacy within our relationships.

Nurturing forgiveness and understanding: When we laugh at our own mistakes and shortcomings, it becomes easier to forgive ourselves and others. This playful approach encourages us to see mistakes as learning opportunities rather than failures, fostering understanding and compassion within our relationships.

Celebrating uniqueness and individuality: In a world that strives for uniformity, embracing our imperfections allows us to celebrate each other's uniqueness and individuality. By acknowledging and appreciating our quirky differences, we create a space for everyone to feel seen, heard, and valued for who they truly are.

Promoting growth and learning: When we share our reverse mantras, we invite others to offer their perspectives and insights. This open dialogue can lead to new discoveries and insights, helping us to challenge our own limiting beliefs and grow as individuals. This shared exploration of self-awareness strengthens our relationships and cultivates a sense of mutual support and development.

By incorporating the practice of reverse mantras into your relationships, you can embark on a journey of deeper connection and genuine understanding. You can create a space for vulnerability, encourage authenticity, and foster a sense of camaraderie. Remember, the most meaningful relationships are not built upon perfection, but upon the shared experience of being human, with all our flaws and imperfections. So, go ahead, share your reverse mantras, laugh at your quirks, and watch your relationships blossom with a newfound depth and strength.

7.Living a more fulfilling life:

In our pursuit of "perfect" lives, we often get entangled in a web of self-doubt and relentless striving. We chase unattainable ideals, compare ourselves to curated online personas, and constantly fret about falling short. This relentless pressure can leave us feeling unfulfilled, disconnected from ourselves, and afraid to truly embrace life. But what if the key to a more fulfilling existence lies not in achieving perfection, but in letting go of it altogether?

This is where the transformative practice of embracing imperfection comes in. By acknowledging and even celebrating our flaws, quirks, and limitations, we break free from the shackles of self-doubt and open ourselves to a world of possibilities. This shift in perspective isn't about self-deprecation, but about self-acceptance, and it can pave the way for a life filled with greater joy, meaning, and fulfillment.

Here are some ways embracing imperfection can unlock a more fulfilling life:

Breaking the comparison Trap: Social media and societal pressures bombard us with images of "perfect" lives, fueling the dangerous game of comparison. Embracing imperfection allows us to step off the comparison treadmill. We recognize that everyone has flaws, and that comparing ourselves to others is a futile and self-defeating exercise. This frees us to focus on our own unique journey and find fulfillment in our individual strengths and passions.

Cultivating self-compassion: We are often our own harshest critics, judging and berating ourselves for every perceived misstep. Embracing imperfection fosters a sense of self-compassion. We learn to laugh at our quirks, forgive our mistakes, and see ourselves as worthy of love and acceptance, flaws and all. This self-compassion is the foundation of true inner peace and a key ingredient for a fulfilling life.

Conquering the fear of failure: The fear of failure can paralyze us, preventing us from taking risks and pursuing our dreams. Embracing imperfection takes the sting out of failure. We see it as a natural part of the learning process, not a reflection of our worth. This reduces our fear of stumbling and empowers us to take bold steps towards our goals, opening doors to new and fulfilling experiences.

Unlocking creativity: Striving for perfection can stifle creativity. We become afraid to experiment, explore, and express ourselves authentically. Embracing imperfection allows us to let go of these constraints. We embrace the messy, the unconventional, and the unexpected. This playful spirit unlocks our creative potential and leads to new ideas, projects, and ways of expressing ourselves, enriching our lives in countless ways.

Deepening connections: In a world obsessed with facades and curated online personas, true connection can be elusive. Embracing imperfection allows us to be vulnerable and authentic with others. We share our struggles, anxieties, and quirks, and in doing so, we invite deeper connection. This vulnerability fosters empathy, understanding, and a sense of belonging, enriching our relationships and making life more meaningful.

Embracing the Present Moment: The pursuit of perfection often keeps us fixated on the future, anxious about achieving some ideal state. Embracing imperfection allows us to let go of this constant striving and appreciate the present moment. We find joy in the small things, the laughter shared with loved ones, the beauty of a sunrise, the simple act of being alive. This present-moment awareness enriches our lives and makes every experience more fulfilling.

Redefining success: Society often defines success by external markers like wealth, status, or achievement. Embracing imperfection allows us to redefine success for ourselves. We focus on personal growth, learning, and living a life aligned with our values. We celebrate our small victories and find fulfillment in the journey itself, not just the destination. This shift in perspective leads to a more meaningful and fulfilling life.

Embracing change and growth: Life is a constant process of change and growth. Embracing imperfection allows us to see challenges and setbacks not as failures, but as opportunities to learn and evolve. We become more resilient, adaptable, and open to new experiences. This willingness to embrace change keeps life exciting, fulfilling, and full of potential.

Finding joy in the imperfect: Imperfection is not something to be hidden or fixed. It is a part of who we are, and it adds a unique texture and richness to our lives. Embracing imperfection allows us to find humor and joy in the unexpected, the messy, and the unconventional. This playful spirit brings lightheartedness and laughter into our lives, making them more enjoyable and fulfilling.

Leaving a Legacy of authenticity: When we embrace our imperfections and live authentically, we inspire others to do the same. We show them that it is okay to be human, to make mistakes, and to be vulnerable. This creates a ripple effect of self-acceptance and empowers others to live their own lives to the fullest. In doing so, we leave a legacy of authenticity and inspire a world where everyone can embrace their unique imperfections and live a life truly fulfilled

8.Contributing to a more positive world:

The ripple effect of self-kindness: building a more positive world

In a world often consumed by negativity and self-criticism, the quiet revolution of self-kindness might seem insignificant. But what if I told you that the way we talk to ourselves isn't just an internal dialogue, but a pebble dropped into a pond, sending ripples outward, affecting those around us and ultimately shaping the world we live in?

Imagine if, instead of berating ourselves for every misstep and dwelling on our flaws, we embraced a practice of reverse mantras. These playful exaggerations of our perceived limitations, laced with humor and acceptance, become tools for self-compassion. They disarm our inner critic and allow us to step out of the self-judgment spiral, radiating a new kind of energy.

This shift in our internal dialogue has the potential to create a powerful ripple effect:

A World of Laughter and Connection: When we laugh at ourselves, we invite others to do the same. This shared laughter breaks down barriers, fosters connection, and creates a more human and relatable atmosphere. In a world yearning for genuine connection, the simple act of laughing together can pave the way for deeper understanding and empathy.

A culture of acceptance and support: By accepting our own imperfections, we open the door for others to do the same. We create a space where vulnerability and authenticity are not weaknesses, but strengths. This shift towards acceptance fosters a more supportive and encouraging environment, where individuals feel empowered to be themselves without fear of judgment.

A surge in self-compassion and resilience: When we practice self-kindness, it becomes easier to extend that same compassion to others. We see mistakes as opportunities for growth, setbacks as temporary bumps on the road, and challenges as opportunities to build resilience. This collective mindset shift leads to a more supportive and understanding world, where individuals are better equipped to navigate life's inevitable difficulties.

A spark of creativity and innovation: Self-compassion fosters a sense of freedom and liberation. Unburdened by the weight of self-criticism, we become more open to experimentation, exploration, and risk-taking. This fertile ground for creativity leads to innovative solutions, groundbreaking ideas, and a world filled with diverse perspectives and expressions.

A decrease in judgment and prejudice: When we focus on our own imperfections, we have less space to judge others for theirs. Embracing self-kindness dismantles the us-versus-them mentality, replacing it with a recognition of our shared humanity. This shift can chip away at prejudice, discrimination, and division, fostering a more inclusive and harmonious world.

A commitment to growth and learning: Self-compassion isn't about complacency; it's about creating a foundation for growth. By accepting ourselves as we are, with flaws and all, we open ourselves to learning and improvement. This commitment to personal development translates into a collective striving for a better future, where individuals are constantly seeking ways to learn, evolve, and contribute positively to the world.

The ripple effect of self-kindness starts with a simple shift in our internal dialogue. By choosing humor and acceptance over self-criticism, we create a space for ourselves and others to flourish. This creates a world where laughter echoes through streets, where vulnerability is met with understanding, and where imperfections are celebrated as unique expressions of our humanity.

So, the next time you catch yourself berating yourself for a misstep, remember the pebble in the pond. Choose a playful reverse mantra, laugh at your quirks, and step into the world with self-compassion. Together, let's create a world where kindness and acceptance ripple outward, transforming not just ourselves, but the very fabric of our shared reality.

Remember, the most powerful revolutions often begin with the smallest whisper. The whisper of self-kindness, amplified by the laughter of shared humanity, can transform the world, one pebble, one ripple at a time.

9.Embracing the journey:

Embracing the journey: Where laughter paves the path to self-discovery

In a world obsessed with optimizing, perfecting, and achieving, the idea of embracing a practice that celebrates imperfection might seem counterintuitive. Yet, nestled within the playful realm of reverse mantras lies a revolutionary tool for embarking on a transformative journey of self-discovery.

Imagine, instead of battling your inner critic with self-flagellation, you disarm it with a playful exaggeration of your perceived flaws. "My procrastination skills are so legendary, I could turn a five-minute task into a five-year Netflix marathon!" This lighthearted absurdity disrupts the critic's power, allowing you to laugh at yourself and step outside the cycle of self-judgment.

This playful shift in perspective is the gateway to a profound journey. By embracing reverse mantras, you embark on a path of:

Self-acceptance, not self-correction: You move away from the relentless pursuit of a "perfect" self and embrace the unique tapestry of your flaws and strengths. You learn to see your quirks and anxieties not as obstacles, but as brushstrokes that add texture and depth to your personal canvas.

Laughter, not lament: You trade the heavy burden of self-criticism for the liberating lightness of laughter. You discover the power of humor to disarm negativity, foster connection, and open the door to self-compassion. When you laugh at yourself, you create space for others to do the same, paving the way for a more authentic and connected world.

Limiting belief demolition, not dogma building: You challenge the rigid narratives your inner critic whispers. "I'm not creative?" becomes, "My creativity is so subtle, it disguises itself as procrastination!" This playful defiance dismantles limiting beliefs, allowing you to explore new possibilities and embrace the full spectrum of your potential.

Growth, not goals: You shed the pressure of achieving specific milestones and step into a continuous process of learning and evolving. You see challenges as opportunities to discover your resilience, and setbacks as detours leading to unexpected destinations. This growth mindset fuels a lifelong journey of self-discovery, where the focus is on becoming, not achieving.

Authenticity, not performance: You let go of the masks and facades society expects you to wear. You embrace your quirks, vulnerabilities, and passions, allowing your true self to shine through. This vulnerability fosters genuine connection and empowers others to do the same, creating a more authentic and inclusive world.

Experimentation, not expectation: You abandon the rigid scripts and predetermined paths. You embrace the unknown, experiment with new ideas, and allow your curiosity to guide the way. This playful exploration leads to unexpected discoveries, hidden talents, and a life brimming with rich experiences.

Embracing the journey of reverse mantras is not about arriving at a specific destination. It's about the dance itself. It's about laughing at the stumbles, celebrating the triumphs, and savoring the ever-changing landscape of your inner world.

So, as you embark on this adventure, remember:

Playfulness is your passport: approach your journey with a light heart and a mischievous spirit. Let laughter be your compass, guiding you to unexpected discoveries and hidden treasures.

Experimentation is your fuel: Don't be afraid to try new mantras, explore different avenues, and rewrite the script of your self-narrative. The more you experiment, the more you'll discover the unique rhythm of your personal journey.

Vulnerability is your strength: Sharing your struggles and imperfections with others is not a weakness, it's a bridge to deeper connection and understanding. In vulnerability lies the power to inspire and be inspired.

Growth is your reward: Focus on the process of becoming, not the pressure of achieving. Celebrate the small wins, learn from the stumbles, and embrace the continuous evolution that defines the journey of self-discovery.

The practice of reverse mantras is not just a tool for self-improvement; it's a revolution in self-acceptance. It's a playful rebellion against the tyranny of perfectionism, an invitation to laugh at ourselves and each other, and a celebration of the messy, beautiful journey of becoming who we truly are. So, take a step into the unknown, embrace the absurdity, and discover the transformative power of laughter and self-compassion. You might just surprise yourself with the hidden potential that lies within.

Remember, the most fulfilling journeys are not those with a predetermined destination, but those guided by the light of laughter, the fuel of curiosity, and the strength of vulnerability. Embrace the journey, dear seeker, and let your reverse mantras light the way.

The "meh" button: Your antidote to petty dramas

Life, in all its glorious messiness, throws a constant barrage of annoyances our way. From the burnt toast in the morning to the passive-aggressive office email, these minor irritations can chip away at our serenity, leaving us feeling frazzled and frustrated. But what if there was a secret weapon, a mental "meh" button we could press to instantly deflect these petty dramas and reclaim our inner peace?

Introducing the "meh" button, your personal force field against the onslaught of everyday annoyances. It's not a physical button, mind you, but rather a mental state, a shift in perspective that allows you to say, "This doesn't deserve my energy," and move on with your day.

Think of it like this: when you encounter a minor annoyance, your brain automatically activates a fight-or-flight response. You get flustered, anxious, maybe even a little angry. The "meh" button, however, is like a giant, cosmic pause button. It interrupts this automatic reaction and allows you to assess the situation with a cool head.

Here's how it works:

1. Recognize the trigger: The first step is to become aware of your own triggers. What are the little things that send your internal alarm system into overdrive? Burnt toast? Traffic jams? A colleague's incessant humming? Once you identify your triggers, you can start to anticipate them and deploy the "meh" button before they hijack your day.

2. Disengage the drama: When you feel the familiar irritation rising, take a deep breath. Instead of letting it consume you, step back mentally. Ask yourself, "Is this really worth my emotional energy?" In most cases, the answer will be a resounding "meh."

3. Hit the "meh" button: Now comes the fun part. Imagine a big, red button labeled "meh" right in the center of your mind. As you visualize it, let the feeling of indifference wash over you. Say "meh" out loud, if you like, with increasing conviction. Feel it vibrate through your core, dissolving the tension and frustration.

4. Reframe the situation: Look at the situation from a different angle. Is that burnt toast a cosmic disaster, or just a minor inconvenience? Is the office hum a personal affront, or simply someone else's quirk? Reframing helps you see things in their proper perspective, shrinking the annoyance and restoring your sense of calm.

5. Shift your focus: Don't let the annoyance dwell in your mind like a bad smell. Redirect your attention to something else, something positive, something that brings you joy. Maybe it's a funny video, a conversation with a loved one, or simply focusing on the beauty of the clouds. Shift your focus, and the annoyance will fade away.

Remember, the "meh" button is not about apathy or ignoring problems. It's about recognizing what deserves your energy and what doesn't. It's about choosing to not be swept away by every minor current in the river of life.

Here are some additional tips for mastering the "meh" button:

Practice makes perfect: The more you use the "meh" button, the easier it will become. Train your brain to see annoyances as "meh-worthy" and your inner peace will soar.

Humor is your secret weapon: Laughter is a powerful antidote to stress and annoyance. Find the humor in the situation, even if it's just a little chuckle to yourself.

Don't be afraid to walk away: If something is truly draining your energy, don't hesitate to remove yourself from the situation. Take a walk, call a friend, do whatever it takes to create space and recharge your "meh" reserves.

Remember, you're in control: You have the power to choose how you react to every situation. Don't let petty dramas dictate your mood or your day. Hit the "meh" button and reclaim your inner peace, one annoyance at a time.

The "meh" button is a simple tool with a profound impact. It's your shield against petty dramas, your ticket to a calmer, more resilient you. So, embrace the "meh," dear reader, and let it guide you towards a life where minor annoyances fade into the background, leaving you free to focus on what truly matters – your joy, your peace, and the ever-unfolding adventure of being alive.

Remember, life is too precious to waste on petty dramas. Hit the "meh" button, laugh at life's little hiccups, and reclaim your right to a life filled with serenity and joy.

Part 3: adventures in brain hacking (the science behind the laughter)

Chapter 7: the chemical imbalance blues:

A hilarious harmony of mood molecules

Ah, the brain. A magnificent, squishy marvel, capable of conjuring symphonies of thought and orchestrating ballets of emotion. But sometimes, this chemical orchestra gets a little out of tune, leaving us humming the blues of a serotonin symphony and the off-key tango of dopamine deficiency. Don't worry, fellow neurotransmitter-challenged souls, for we're about to dive into the wacky world of brain chemistry, where laughter and understanding join hands to demystify the "chemical imbalance blues."

Imagine your brain as a vibrant nightclub, pulsating with the energy of neurotransmitters. Serotonin, the sassy chanteuse, struts across the stage, belting out tunes of happiness and contentment. Dopamine, the charismatic dj, spins the discs of motivation and reward, keeping the party groovin'. And then there's the introverted bouncer, gaba, who chills in the corner, keeping things calm and collected.

But sometimes, these star performers get a little tipsy. Serotonin might drown her sorrows in a bottomless mimosa of sadness, leaving us feeling like wallflowers at a party we didn't want to attend. Dopamine, the party animal, might crash after a bender of excessive stimulation, leaving us feeling like we've danced too hard and now our enthusiasm's gone limp.

And gaba? Well, gaba might have accidentally spiked the punch bowl with a little too much chill, turning the nightclub into a library, and our brains into sleepy sloths.

These chemical imbalances can manifest in a variety of ways. The serotonin slump can leave us feeling blue, unmotivated, and craving carbs like a lost penguin in a bakery. Dopamine deficiency might turn us into productivity zombies, staring at our to-do lists with the same enthusiasm as a hamster on a treadmill. And gaba's overzealousness can leave us feeling like we're wading through treacle, with thoughts moving at the speed of a snail on a sleeping pill.

But fear not, for the "chemical imbalance blues" don't have to be a permanent gig. We can be the roadies of our own brains, tuning the chemical orchestra back to harmony. Here's how:

Serotonin serenade: get your sunshine on! Sunlight boosts serotonin production, so soak up those rays like a lizard on a hot rock. Exercise is another serotonin booster, so get your groove on, whether it's a disco dance party in your living room or a jog around the block. And don't forget the power of gratitude. Counting your blessings, even the silly ones (like having eyebrows that aren't permanently surprised), can give serotonin a little pep talk.

Dopamine disco: break the monotony! Novelty is dopamine's jam, so shake things up a bit. Learn a new skill, take a spontaneous adventure, or even rearrange your furniture. Accomplishing small tasks can also give dopamine a mini-disco party, so check things off your to-do list like you're dj-ing your own life remix.

Gaba groove: chill out, bro. Meditation is like a spa day for your brain, calming gaba and quieting the inner chatter. Deep breathing is another gaba-friendly groove, so inhale peace, exhale stress. And don't underestimate the power of a good laugh. Laughter is like a gaba-infused cocktail, melting away tension and leaving you feeling light and bubbly.

Remember, the "chemical imbalance blues" are just a temporary riff in the grand symphony of your life. With a little understanding, humor, and some self-care tunes, you can get your neurotransmitters back in sync and dance your way to a happier, more fulfilling you. So put on your metaphorical headphones, crank up the volume on self-compassion, and let the laughter wash away the blues. After all, the brain's chemical orchestra is yours to conduct. So maestro, grab your baton and start composing the music of your joy!

...and stay tuned for next subject, where we'll delve into the fascinating world of gut bacteria and their surprising influence on our mental well-being. Get ready for a hilarious exploration of the "microbiome mambo"!

The chemical imbalance blues: encore! A deep dive into the gut-brain tango and beyond

We've dipped our toes in the wacky world of brain chemistry and the hidden symphony of gut bacteria, but the "chemical imbalance blues" have even more instruments in their orchestra. Let's grab some noise-canceling headphones and delve deeper into the hidden dimensions of our emotional landscape.

The sleep symphony: while we drift off to dreamland, our brains aren't exactly resting. They're composing a nocturnal symphony of hormones and neurotransmitters that orchestrates our mood, energy levels, and cognitive function. Sleep deprivation, the cranky conductor of this orchestra, throws everything out of whack. Serotonin dips, cortisol (the anxiety anthem) blares too loud, and cognitive clarity gets lost in a cacophony of foggy thoughts. But fear not, insomniacs! With a few adjustments to your sleep hygiene, you can turn your slumber into a lullaby of well-being:

Dimming the lights: a pre-sleep ritual for digital detox and dreamland

In the ever-illuminated world we've created, sleep often feels like a fickle guest, easily spooked by the blue-tinged glare of our devices. This digital dawn casts a long shadow, suppressing our natural sleep hormone, melatonin, and leaving us tossing and turning, yearning for the embrace of slumber. But fret not, fellow weary souls, for a simple act of rebellion offers a potent antidote: dimming the stage lights.

Imagine your bedroom as a cozy theater, bathed in the warm glow of anticipation. The bed, a plush stage, awaits the star of the show – you. But alas, the villain, the blue light emanating from your phone, bathes the room in a sterile, digital chill. Melatonin, the sleep fairy, huddles in the shadows, her lullaby unheard amidst the digital din. The audience, your mind and body, remain restless, their desire for sleep thwarted by the artificial light.

But with a simple twist of the dimmer switch, the scene transforms. Candlelight paints the walls in warm, honeyed tones, casting dancing shadows that whisper promises of slumber. The blue light monster shrinks, its digital grip loosening as the stage dims. Melatonin, sensing her chance, steps into the spotlight, her gentle hum washing over the room like a wave of peace.

This pre-sleep ritual, this dimming of the digital sun, is more than just a sleep hygiene tip; it's a conscious choice. It's a reclamation of the darkness that cradles sleep, a return to the primal rhythm where our ancestors navigated by the moon's gentle sway. It's a rebellion against the tyranny of the ever-lit screen, a declaration of allegiance to the restorative power of darkness.

As twilight descends, resist the hypnotic pull of your phone. Let the notifications wait, the emails rest. Instead, light a candle, its flickering flame a beacon against the digital tide. Curl up with a book, its pages whispering tales of faraway dreams. Or, step outside, and let the starlight bathe you in its celestial lullaby.

Feel the tension melt away as the light dims. Your body, no longer subjected to the blue light's frenetic energy, begins its descent into the valley of sleep. Melatonin, empowered by the darkness, weaves its magic, lulling you into a state of blissful slumber.

For it is in the dimness that sleep finds its stage. The anxieties that plagued you recede into the shadows, the digital noise fades to a gentle hum, and the orchestra of your dreams begins its enchanting performance.

So, embrace the darkness, dear traveler. Let the stage lights dim, and step into your own personal haven of slumber. For within that quiet hush lies the gateway to a night of restorative sleep, a sanctuary where your mind and body can truly rest and renew. Remember, you are the conductor of your own slumber symphony. Dim the lights, silence the digital noise, and let the stars guide you into the arms of a restful sleep.

Sweet dreams.

Silence the loudmouths: orchestrating a symphony of sleep in a noisy world

Ah, sleep. That elusive maestro of our nightly orchestra, weaving melodies of rest and rejuvenation. But alas, like any concert, our slumber symphony can be disrupted by unwanted guests – the cacophony of noise pollution, the uninvited percussionists in the orchestra of our dreams. From the honking horns of the city to the snoring roommate's aria, these disruptive elements can leave us tossing and turning, yearning for the sweet silence of dreamland.

But fear not, fellow sleep-seekers! For just like a skilled conductor, we can silence the loudmouths and reclaim the stage of our slumber. Let us wield the tools of noise-cancelling magic, and transform the symphony of the city into a lullaby of serenity.

Firstly, consider the earplugs, the quiet warriors of our sleep arsenal. These tiny shields, like miniature soundproof booths, block out the unwanted noise, allowing the calming hum of your own breath to take center stage. Imagine them as velvet curtains drawn across the windows of your mind, shutting out the honking horns and traffic rumbles.

Next, enter the white noise machine, the gentle giant of our sleep symphony. This sonic sorcerer, through its soothing hum or rhythmic whoosh, drowns out the disruptive melodies of the outside world. Think of it as a nature documentary playing on repeat, the crashing waves or rustling leaves lulling your anxieties to sleep.

And for the truly light sleepers, there's the sleep mask, the silent sentinel of our slumber. This velvety shield, worn like a blindfold for dreams, plunges your world into darkness, severing the visual cues that might trigger unwanted wakefulness. Picture it as a blackout curtain for your mind, blocking out the streetlights and flickering screens, leaving only the soft whispers of your own imagination.

But silencing the external noise is only half the melody. The true magic lies in quieting the internal cacophony, the anxieties and worries that keep us up, like a blaring saxophone solo in our sleep orchestra. For this, we must turn inward, practicing calming techniques like deep breathing or meditation. Imagine them as oboes and flutes, weaving a countermelody of peace that harmonizes with the soothing white noise or the gentle hum of earplugs.

Remember, silencing the loudmouths is not about isolating yourself from the world, but about creating a haven for sleep within it. It's about claiming your right to a restful night, a sanctuary where the only music playing is the lullaby of your own breath and the symphony of your dreams.

So, dear sleep-seeker, as the city lights dim and the world prepares for its nightly chorus, do not despair. Invest in the tools of noise-cancelling magic, embrace the quiet power of darkness, and silence the loudmouths within your own mind. For in the stillness, you will find the stage for your own sleep symphony, a conductor's baton waiting to be wielded. And when the last note of the city's lullaby fades, you will rise, refreshed and rejuvenated, ready to face the day with a melody of peace still humming in your heart.

Sweet dreams, dear sleeper. May your slumber be a symphony of silence, orchestrated by the maestro of your own well-being.

Set the mood: transforming your bedroom into a slumber sanctuary

As dusk paints the sky with its twilight brushstrokes, most of us yearn for the sanctuary of sleep, a haven where our minds and bodies can unwind and recharge. But too often, our bedrooms resemble chaotic battlegrounds, cluttered with work emails and to-do lists, the very antithesis of restful slumber.

Yet, fear not, weary traveler, for within your four walls lies the potential for a transformative symphony of sleep – a space that whispers of relaxation and invites you into the arms of morpheus.

Imagine your bedroom as an orchestra hall, not for the cacophony of anxieties, but for the gentle lullaby of rest. The first step in setting the mood is to clear the stage, to banish the clutter of the day. Pack away work emails, fold laundry, and tidy up surfaces. Let go of the unfinished business, knowing it will wait for you refreshed in the light of dawn.

Next, dim the lights, the spotlight of your slumber symphony. Replace harsh overhead bulbs with soft lamps that bathe the room in warm, amber hues. Think flickering candles, casting dancing shadows on the walls, or fairy lights strung like constellations across the ceiling.

Now, introduce the scent of serenity. A gentle spritz of lavender essential oil or a diffuser releasing the calming aroma of chamomile can work wonders. These fragrant whispers create an atmosphere of tranquility, preparing your mind and body for the descent into sleep.

And lastly, let music be the conductor of your slumber. But ditch the blaring beats and opt for gentle instrumentals, like the soft piano melodies of debussy or the soothing cello vibrations of bach. These sonic therapists will lull your anxieties to sleep, replacing them with a sense of peace and quiet contentment.

As you settle into your sanctuary, embrace the rituals that signal the end of your waking act. A warm bath, a gentle stretch, a few pages of a calming book – each act a brushstroke in the canvas of your sleep symphony. Disconnect from the digital world, letting the glow of screens fade into the darkness.

Remember, setting the mood is not about achieving a pinterest-perfect aesthetic, but about creating a space that resonates with your soul. Experiment with different scents, textures, and sounds until you discover the perfect harmony that invites you into the embrace of slumber.

For in that quietude, in the dimmed light and the lullaby of music, your bedroom transforms from a mere room into a refuge. It becomes a haven for self-care, a stage for your own personal sleep symphony where anxieties melt away and dreams take flight. So, dear sleep-seeker, step into your sanctuary, let the world fade away, and embrace the transformative power of setting the mood. For within that quiet space lies the gateway to a night of restful sleep, a journey towards a more rejuvenated and peaceful you.

Sweet dreams, dear friend. May your bedroom be a symphony of tranquility, and your sleep, a lullaby of peace.

Move it before you snooze: orchestrating a pre-sleep concerto for rest

As the sun dips below the horizon, painting the sky in hues of slumber, our bodies begin to crave the sweet embrace of sleep. Yet, for many of us, the transition from wakefulness to rest can be a bumpy ride, filled with anxieties and restless limbs. But fear not, weary travelers, for within the realm of pre-sleep rituals lies a secret weapon – the harmonious melody of movement.

Think of your body as a grand orchestra, its muscles and mind instruments waiting to be tuned. Exercise, that gentle maestro, can warm up this orchestra, preparing it for the grand finale of sleep. But just like any conductor, we must choose the right notes to play, for bicep curls in the twilight are hardly the prelude to slumber.

Instead, let's turn the volume down on the high-energy routines and embrace the gentle whispers of movement. Imagine a moonlit walk, where each step is a brushstroke on the canvas of the night, releasing tension with every stride. Or picture a yoga practice, the soft stretching and flowing sequences like a lullaby for your muscles, coaxing them into a state of calm surrender.

Even a few minutes of mindful movement can work wonders. Imagine a simple sun salutation, the slow rise and fall of your body echoing the rhythm of the setting sun. Or picture a gentle neck roll, releasing the tension that often gathers there like a weary traveler. These quiet movements, like whispers in the night, prepare your body for the journey into sleep, leaving it relaxed and ready to drift off.

But the magic of pre-sleep movement extends beyond the physical. As you move, your mind, too, feels the rhythm. Anxious thoughts, like unruly percussionists, begin to quiet, replaced by the gentle hum of focus. The worries that once dominated your inner stage fade into the background, replaced by the melody of your breath and the soft whispers of your body.

Remember, dear sleep-seeker, the key is to move with intention, not intensity. This is not a high-octane workout, but a gentle concerto for your mind and body. Listen to your intuition, let your body guide you, and choose movements that resonate with your soul.

For within this pre-sleep dance lies a transformative power. It's a way to release the day's residue, to quiet the anxieties that keep us tossing and turning. It's a way to prepare our orchestra for the final act of sleep, creating a stage where dreams can take flight and rest can wash over us like a lullaby.

So, as the day reaches its crescendo and the world prepares for its nightly slumber, step onto the stage of your own pre-sleep ritual. Let your body move to the gentle rhythm of the evening, and allow the melody of movement to guide you towards the embrace of sleep. For in that quiet space, where your breath and movement harmonize, lies the gateway to a night of restorative slumber, a symphony of rest where you can truly recharge and awaken anew.

Sweet dreams, dear friend. May your pre-sleep movements be a lullaby for your body and a serenade for your soul.

Embrace the ritual: orchestrating a lullaby for your mind and body

As the world dims and day surrenders to the embrace of twilight, our bodies yearn for the sweet melody of sleep. Yet, for many of us, the journey from wakefulness to slumber is fraught with restlessness and anxieties, a chaotic prelude to the much-desired finale. But fear not, weary travelers, for within the quietude lies a secret weapon - the harmonious ritual of winding down.

Think of your mind and body as a grand orchestra, its instruments poised and ready. Bedtime rituals, like a gentle conductor, can guide this orchestra towards the restful finale of sleep. These rituals, like brushstrokes on the canvas of your evening, create a consistent pattern, a lullaby that signals to your brain it's time to wind down.

Imagine a warm bath, a steamy haven where worries dissolve like wisps of mist. Picture the soft glow of candles, their flickering flames casting dancing shadows that chase away anxieties. Feel the gentle caress of the water, a soothing balm that washes away the day's tension, leaving your muscles humming with peace.

Or picture the quiet hum of a book, its pages whispering tales of faraway dreams. Let the words flow like a gentle stream, carrying your thoughts away from the day's worries and towards the tranquil shores of sleep. As each sentence unfolds, feel your eyelids grow heavy, your mind lulled into a state of quiet contentment.

Perhaps a journal beckons, a confidante waiting to absorb the day's anxieties. Let your worries flow onto the page, ink becoming a conduit for release. As you pen your thoughts, feel them lose their grip, their power fading with each stroke of the pen. Close the book, leaving your anxieties behind, and step into the embrace of slumber unburdened.

But remember, dear traveler, the magic lies not in the specific ritual, but in the consistency. Choose practices that resonate with your soul, that paint your own unique lullaby on the canvas of your evening. Whether it's a quiet cup of chamomile tea, a soothing stretch, or a whispered conversation with your loved ones, let your rituals become the gentle threads that weave your pathway to sleep.

For in this consistency lies the power of the lullaby. As your brain recognizes the familiar patterns, the soft hum of your rituals, it begins to relax, releasing the day's grip. Anxieties quiet, worries fade, and the orchestra of your mind and body falls into a harmonious slumber symphony.

So, as the sun dips below the horizon, embrace the power of ritual. Let your evening unfold in a sequence of quietude, each act a brushstroke towards the restful finale. For within these simple practices lies the gateway to a night of restorative sleep, a haven where your mind and body can truly surrender to the lullaby of slumber.

Sweet dreams, dear friend. May your rituals be a gentle serenade for your soul, guiding you towards the embrace of a peaceful, rejuvenating sleep.

Remember, sleep is not just a passive state; it's an active process that plays a vital role in our emotional well-being. By becoming the conductor of your sleep symphony, you can silence the "chemical imbalance blues" and wake up feeling refreshed, energized, and ready to face the day with a smile.

The inflammation interlude: inflammation, the pesky percussionist in the orchestra of our health, can also contribute to the "chemical imbalance blues." chronic inflammation, often triggered by stress, diet, or even environmental factors, can disrupt the delicate balance of our neurotransmitters, leading to mood swings, anxiety, and fatigue. But this fiery interlude doesn't have to ruin the whole performance:

Fuel the firefighters: omega-3 fatty acids found in fatty fish, nuts, and seeds are like firefighters for inflammation. They help to dampen the flames and promote cellular repair. Think of them as cool jazz to your body's fiery salsa.

Spice up your life (the right way): turmeric, ginger, and garlic are nature's anti-inflammatory wonders. These culinary maestros contain curcumin, gingerols, and allicin, powerful compounds that can help reduce inflammation and soothe your internal orchestra.

Stress less, breathe more: chronic stress is like a conductor on a sugar rush, cranking up the volume on inflammation. Techniques like meditation, deep breathing, and spending time in nature can help you downshift and bring the internal fire under control.

Sleep tight, inflammation takes flight: remember our sleep symphony? Getting enough quality sleep helps regulate your immune system and reduce inflammation. So, dim the stage lights, silence the noisemakers, and let your body use the night to repair and restore balance.

By taming the flames of inflammation, you can create a more harmonious inner environment, where your neurotransmitters can sing their happy tunes and your mood can soar like a well-rehearsed finale.

The mind-body chorus: we've journeyed through the gut-brain tango, the sleep symphony, and the inflammation interlude, but the "chemical imbalance blues" have one more act in their repertoire: the mind-body chorus. Our thoughts and emotions are not just abstract concepts; they are physical entities, influencing the chemical landscape of our brains and bodies. Negative self-talk, rumination, and chronic stress act like discordant backing vocals, throwing the whole chorus off-key. But there are also instruments of positivity waiting to be played:

Gratitude's gentle melody: cultivating gratitude, like humming a happy tune, releases a wave of positive neurotransmitters.

Chapter 8: harnessing the transformative power of play:

Unlocking the science behind laughter and playfulness

Welcome to chapter 8 of your self-help journey, where we dive deep into the extraordinary realm of play and laughter. In this chapter, we'll explore how these seemingly simple acts can have profound effects on your well-being and offer practical exercises to help you incorporate more playfulness into your life.

Understanding the science behind playfulness: the endorphin-fueled joy of being playful

Playfulness is often associated with carefree childhood days, but it's a mistake to think that it's something we outgrow as adults. In fact, play is an integral part of human nature that continues to benefit us throughout our lives. Whether it's a game of tag with friends, a spontaneous dance party in the living room, or a playful banter with colleagues, engaging in playful activities has a profound impact on our physical and mental well-being. Let's delve into the science behind playfulness and explore how it triggers the release of endorphins—the magical feel-good chemicals that reduce stress and promote happiness.

Endorphins, often referred to as the body's natural painkillers, are neurotransmitters produced by the central nervous system and pituitary gland. They play a key role in regulating mood, reducing pain, and promoting feelings of pleasure and well-being. When we engage in activities that bring us joy and excitement, such as play, our brains reward us by releasing a flood of these delightful endorphins.

So, what exactly happens in our brains when we're being playful? Picture this: you're engaged in a game of frisbee with friends on a sunny afternoon. As you run, jump, and laugh, your brain is hard at work, releasing endorphins into your bloodstream. These endorphins bind to specialized receptors in your brain, triggering a cascade of physiological responses that leave you feeling on top of the world.

One of the most common expressions of playfulness is laughter. Whether it's a hearty belly laugh or a contagious giggle fit, laughter is like a supercharged turbo boost for our endorphin levels. When we laugh, our bodies undergo a series of changes that further enhance the effects of endorphins. Muscles relax, tension dissipates, and blood flow increases, leading to a sense of relaxation and well-being.

But laughter doesn't just make us feel good in the moment—it also has long-lasting benefits for our health and happiness. Studies have shown that laughter can boost the immune system, reduce inflammation, and even improve cardiovascular health. It's no wonder that laughter is often called "the best medicine"

So, how can we harness the power of playfulness to reap these incredible benefits in our own lives? The key is to make time for play and prioritize activities that bring us joy and laughter. Whether it's joining a recreational sports team, attending a comedy show, or simply goofing around with friends, finding ways to incorporate play into our daily routines is essential for our overall well-being.

But playfulness isn't just about having fun—it's also about cultivating a mindset of curiosity, creativity, and spontaneity. When we approach life with a playful attitude, we're more open to new experiences, more resilient in the face of challenges, and more connected to those around us. Playfulness encourages us to let go of our inhibitions, embrace our inner child, and fully immerse ourselves in the present moment.

Incorporating playfulness into our lives doesn't have to be complicated or time-consuming. It can be as simple as taking a break to play a quick game of ping pong during lunch, sharing a funny joke with a coworker, or indulging in a hobby that brings us joy. The important thing is to make time for play and prioritize activities that nourish our souls and bring us happiness.

In conclusion, playfulness is a fundamental aspect of human nature that continues to benefit us throughout our lives. When we engage in playful activities, our brains release endorphins—the magical feel-good chemicals that reduce stress and promote happiness. Laughter, a common expression of playfulness, further enhances these effects by relaxing muscles, increasing blood flow, and boosting our mood. By making time for play and embracing a playful mindset, we can unlock the transformative power of playfulness and experience greater joy, connection, and fulfillment in our lives.

But playfulness isn't just about having fun—it's also a powerful tool for building connections and fostering creativity. When we approach life with a playful mindset, we're more open to new experiences, more resilient in the face of challenges, and more connected to those around us. By embracing playfulness, we can cultivate stronger relationships, enhance our problem-solving skills, and infuse our lives with joy and spontaneity.

Now, let's put theory into practice with two simple yet effective exercises:

Negativity charades: take a moment to reflect on the sources of negativity in your life—whether it's stress at work, conflicts with loved ones, or personal insecurities. Then, gather a group of friends or family members and play a game of negativity charades. Each person takes turns acting out a negative scenario without using words, while the others guess what it is. Through this lighthearted exercise, you'll learn to laugh at life's challenges and find creative ways to overcome them.

compliment bonanza: set aside some time each day to express genuine appreciation for yourself and others. Write down three things you admire about yourself and three things you admire about someone else. Then, share these compliments with yourself or the intended recipient. By focusing on the positive qualities in yourself and others, you'll cultivate a mindset of gratitude and strengthen your relationships in the process."

Chapter 9: the relatable rogues' gallery

In the realm of human experience, everyone confronts the inner jerk—the voice of doubt, criticism, or fear that tries to pull us down. This internal adversary, often rooted in past experiences, insecurities, or societal pressures, can be formidable. Yet, countless stories exist of individuals who, through resilience, courage, and creativity, have silenced or befriended their inner critics. Let's explore some of these inspiring journeys, illustrating how real people overcame their inner jerks.

The musician who silenced her inner critic

Tara grew up in a family where music was a way of life. Her parents were both classical musicians, and her older siblings had taken up various instruments. Tara, however, always felt overshadowed by their talent and success. When she started playing the violin, her inner critic was relentless: "you'll never be as good as them," it would say. "why even bother?"

Despite her doubts, tara loved music. She decided to pursue it in her own way, playing for small audiences and participating in local events. However, her inner critic often left her feeling inadequate. It wasn't until she met a supportive mentor who encouraged her to embrace her unique style that things began to change.

Her mentor, a seasoned violinist, shared stories of his own struggles with self-doubt and encouraged tara to focus on her passion rather than comparisons. He taught her that music was about expression, not competition. Gradually, tara learned to silence her inner critic by immersing herself in her music and surrounding herself with positive influences. She found joy in her performances and began to connect with her audiences on a deeper level. Her journey serves as a testament to the power of embracing one's uniqueness to overcome self-doubt.

The entrepreneur who befriended his fear of failure

David always dreamed of starting his own business, but he was haunted by a persistent fear of failure. He had seen many entrepreneurs struggle, and the idea of risking everything for an uncertain outcome terrified him. His inner jerk constantly whispered, "what if you fail? What will people think of you?"

Despite his fears, david decided to take the leap and start his own tech company. He soon discovered that the path to entrepreneurship was filled with challenges and setbacks. His fear of failure intensified with each obstacle, leading to sleepless nights and moments of despair. However, instead of allowing his fear to paralyze him, david decided to befriend it.

He attended workshops and seminars on entrepreneurship and began reading books about successful businesspeople who had faced similar fears. He realized that failure was a common part of the journey and that every setback was an opportunity to learn. David also joined a network of entrepreneurs who shared their stories of overcoming adversity, providing him with a support system that helped him reframe his perspective.

With time, david's fear of failure became a motivator rather than a hindrance. He used it to drive his creativity and innovation, developing products that addressed real-world problems. His business thrived, not because he never experienced failure, but because he learned to embrace it as part of the process. David's story illustrates that when we face our fears and understand their roots, they can become allies in our journey toward success.

the writer who transformed self-doubt into creativity

Emily had always wanted to be a writer, but her inner jerk constantly belittled her ambitions. "your writing isn't good enough," it would tell her. "who would want to read your work?" despite these doubts, emily found solace in writing, using it as a way to express her thoughts and emotions.

As she pursued her dream, emily faced numerous rejections from publishers and literary agents. Each rejection seemed to confirm her inner critic's negative voice, but she refused to let it define her. Instead, emily decided to transform her self-doubt into a source of creativity.

She began writing for herself, focusing on the stories she wanted to tell rather than what she thought others wanted to read. Emily joined a writing group where she received constructive feedback and encouragement. This supportive environment helped her see her writing's potential and gave her the confidence to continue.

Emily's breakthrough came when she self-published a collection of short stories that resonated with readers. The positive response and encouragement from her audience helped her silence her inner critic for good. She continued to write, focusing on authenticity and personal growth rather than seeking validation from traditional publishing channels. Emily's journey is a reminder that creativity often flourishes when we let go of self-doubt and embrace our unique voice.

the athlete who conquered his inner demons

Mark was a promising athlete with dreams of competing at the highest level. However, his inner jerk constantly reminded him of past failures and setbacks. "you'll never make it," it would say. "you're not strong enough." these doubts plagued him during training and competitions, leading to performance anxiety and self-sabotage.

Mark's turning point came when he met a sports psychologist who helped him understand the impact of negative self-talk on his performance. Through therapy and mental training, mark learned to identify the triggers for his inner critic and develop coping strategies. He practiced mindfulness and visualization techniques, focusing on his strengths and achievements rather than his failures.

As mark applied these techniques, he began to see a significant improvement in his performance. He learned to quiet his inner demons by replacing negative thoughts with positive affirmations. This shift in mindset allowed him to compete with confidence and resilience, ultimately leading to a successful career in sports. Mark's story underscores the importance of mental strength and the ability to overcome internal obstacles in the pursuit of excellence.

These stories of real people overcoming their inner jerks highlight the common struggles we all face and the potential for transformation when we confront our inner critics. Whether it's silencing self-doubt, befriending fear, or turning criticism into creativity, the key is to find the strength within ourselves and seek support from those who believe in us. By doing so, we can rise above our inner jerks and achieve remarkable success..

If someone had told me years ago that i would eventually transform my life entirely by overcoming my inner jerk, i would have dismissed it as wishful thinking. Back then, i was entangled in a constant internal battle, with a critical voice that undermined my self-worth and kept me from reaching my full potential. Yet, as i stand here today, i know my story of transformation is real. It was a journey that involved self-reflection, hard work, and a relentless commitment to personal growth.

The rise of my inner jerk

My inner jerk had been a constant companion for as long as i could remember. It started as a subtle whisper, questioning my abilities and decisions. Over time, it grew into a persistent, negative narrative that influenced how i viewed myself and the world around me. In school, i doubted my intelligence and constantly compared myself to others. In relationships, i believed i wasn't good enough, leading me to sabotage them before they could blossom.

This critical inner voice became my default mode of thinking. It was harsh, judgmental, and unforgiving. I often found myself ruminating on past mistakes, replaying negative events, and imagining worst-case scenarios for the future. It affected my career, my social life, and my mental health. Despite achieving certain milestones, the inner jerk always found a way to downplay my successes and emphasize my failures.

the breaking point

The turning point came when i hit rock bottom. I had lost a job i loved due to a series of unfortunate events, and my relationship with my partner ended abruptly. My self-esteem plummeted, and i found myself spiraling into a cycle of self-blame and despair. The inner jerk was louder than ever, telling me that i was worthless and that i would never amount to anything.

It was during this dark period that i realized i couldn't continue living this way. I knew i needed to change, but i wasn't sure where to start. I felt overwhelmed by the magnitude of the transformation i needed to undertake. However, i also knew that if i didn't take action, i would remain trapped in this toxic cycle. I decided to seek help and began attending therapy sessions.

The journey to overcoming my inner jerk

Therapy was the first step in my journey to overcoming my inner jerk. My therapist helped me understand the root causes of my negative self-talk and guided me in identifying the patterns that fueled it. Through cognitive behavioral therapy, i learned how to challenge my negative thoughts and replace them with healthier, more constructive ones.

One of the key exercises my therapist introduced was thought reframing. I began to catch myself when the inner jerk started speaking and consciously reframed those thoughts into positive or neutral ones. For example, when i found myself thinking, "you're a failure," i would counter it with, "you've faced setbacks, but you've also achieved a lot. You can learn from this and grow." this shift in perspective was liberating, as it allowed me to see my experiences through a different lens.

Alongside therapy, i started practicing mindfulness and meditation. These practices helped me become more aware of my thoughts and emotions, allowing me to create distance from the inner jerk's critical voice. Through mindfulness, i developed the ability to observe my thoughts without judgment, which made it easier to challenge and dismiss the negative ones.

Building a support system

As i continued my journey, i realized the importance of surrounding myself with positive influences. I sought out supportive friends and mentors who encouraged me and believed in my potential. They became my sounding boards, offering constructive feedback and reminding me of my strengths when the inner jerk tried to bring me down.

I also distanced myself from toxic relationships and environments that fueled negativity. This was not always easy, as it meant letting go of certain friendships and distancing myself from people who were a source of criticism. However, i knew it was necessary for my mental and emotional well-being.

finding my purpose

With a clearer mind and a stronger support system, i began exploring my passions and interests. I discovered that when i focused on activities that brought me joy and fulfillment, the inner jerk's voice grew quieter. I started volunteering at a local community center, where i could make a positive impact on others. This experience gave me a sense of purpose and helped me realize that my worth wasn't tied to external achievements but to the positive difference i could make in the world.

I also revisited my career goals and took steps to pursue opportunities that aligned with my values. I decided to further my education and acquired new skills that opened doors to a career path i was genuinely excited about. This process wasn't without its challenges, but i learned to view setbacks as opportunities for growth rather than reasons to give up.

the transformation

Overcoming my inner jerk was not an overnight process. It required consistent effort, self-reflection, and the willingness to confront uncomfortable truths. However, as i continued on this journey, i noticed profound changes in my life. I was more confident, resilient, and optimistic about the future. I no longer allowed the inner jerk to dictate my decisions or limit my potential.

The transformation was also evident in my relationships. I formed deeper connections with people who valued me for who i was, not for what i could achieve. I became more compassionate toward myself and others, realizing that everyone has their own inner struggles to overcome.

My journey to overcoming my inner jerk transformed my life in ways i could never have imagined. It was a journey marked by challenges, but also by profound growth and self-discovery. By confronting and silencing my inner critic, i unlocked my potential and found a renewed sense of purpose and fulfillment.

If there's one thing i've learned from this experience, it's that change is possible, no matter how entrenched our inner jerks may be. It requires courage, persistence, and a commitment to personal growth. Most importantly, it requires the belief that we are worthy of living a life free from the constraints of negativity and self-doubt. My story is proof that with determination and the right support, we can all overcome our inner jerks and embrace the best versions of ourselves.

Part 4: a life beyond the jerk (maintaining your mental sunshine)

Chapter 10: the jerk whisperer:

Learn to talk to your inner critic with compassion and understanding, eventually negotiating a truce

In every person's life, there's an inner voice that often finds faults, points out flaws, and questions every move. It's the inner critic, or as some call it, the "inner jerk." for some, it's just an occasional whisper. For others, it's a relentless scream that influences their thoughts, feelings, and decisions. In this chapter, we explore a compassionate approach to addressing this inner critic, aiming not to silence it completely but to negotiate a truce that allows you to live more freely and peacefully.

Understanding the role of the inner critic

Before delving into strategies for talking to your inner critic with compassion, it's crucial to understand its role. The inner critic, despite its abrasive nature, often stems from a protective instinct. It seeks to shield you from embarrassment, failure, or harm. Unfortunately, its methods are counterproductive, relying on fear, shame, and negativity to prevent you from taking risks.

Imagine the inner critic as a character in a play—one who has forgotten its original script and now improvises through a lens of fear and doubt. It is this character that needs guidance and compassion, not eradication.

Why compassion matters

When we approach the inner critic with aggression or suppression, it tends to fight back. The more we resist it, the louder it becomes, like a child throwing a tantrum when ignored. Compassion, on the other hand, offers a different approach. By acknowledging the inner critic's presence and understanding its fears, you can start a dialogue that leads to a more balanced relationship.

Compassion doesn't mean agreeing with everything the inner critic says. Instead, it means recognizing its concerns and addressing them with understanding. This approach can reduce the intensity of the inner critic's attacks, allowing you to move forward with greater confidence and clarity.

The compassionate conversation

To engage in a compassionate conversation with your inner critic, it's helpful to imagine it as a separate entity, like a character in a book or a friend who is struggling. This separation allows you to listen without becoming overwhelmed by its negativity. Here are steps to guide this conversation:

Acknowledge its presence

Start by acknowledging the inner critic's presence. Say to yourself, "i hear you, and i understand that you're trying to protect me." this simple acknowledgment can diffuse some of the inner critic's power and open the door to a more constructive dialogue.

Ask about its concerns

Inquire about the specific concerns the inner critic has. Ask questions like, "what are you afraid of?" or "what do you think could go wrong?" by exploring these fears, you can gain insights into the underlying beliefs driving the inner critic's behavior.

Express compassion and understanding

After hearing the inner critic's concerns, respond with compassion. You might say, "i understand that you're worried about failure, but it's okay to take risks. We can learn from our mistakes." this compassionate response shows that you're listening and willing to address the concerns without letting them control you.

Negotiate a truce

With a better understanding of the inner critic's fears, you can negotiate a truce. This might involve setting boundaries, like agreeing to give the inner critic a specific time to voice its concerns, but not allowing it to dominate your thoughts throughout the day. You could say, "let's talk about this during our reflection time tonight, but right now, i need to focus on my work."

Offer reassurance

Reassure the inner critic that you value its perspective but that you're in control of your life. You can say, "i appreciate your concern, but i'm capable of making my own decisions. I will take your advice into account, but i also need to follow my intuition."

Putting it into practice

To truly become a jerk whisperer, you need to practice these compassionate conversations regularly. Here are some techniques to help you maintain a healthy relationship with your inner critic:

- journaling

Write down your conversations with the inner critic. This can help you keep track of its concerns and your responses, allowing you to see patterns over time.

- mindfulness

Practice mindfulness to become more aware of your thoughts and feelings. This awareness can help you recognize when the inner critic is speaking and give you the space to respond compassionately.

-affirmation

Create affirmations that counter the inner critic's negative messages. For example, if the inner critic says, "you're not good enough," respond with, "i am capable and deserving of success."

Seek support

If the inner critic becomes overwhelming, seek support from a therapist or counselor. Professional guidance can provide additional tools for managing negative self-talk and building self-compassion.

Learning to talk to your inner critic with compassion and understanding is a transformative journey. By acknowledging its presence, addressing its concerns, and negotiating a truce, you can create a healthier relationship with yourself. This approach doesn't eliminate the inner critic, but it helps you manage its influence, allowing you to live a more fulfilling and empowered life. As you continue to practice these compassionate conversations, you'll find that the inner critic's voice becomes less dominant, and your inner peace grows.

Chapter 11: the laughter lifeline:

Build a network of cheerleaders, humor-loving friends who can help you hit the "meh" button and drown out the negativity with laughter.

Laughter is a powerful antidote to stress, negativity, and isolation. It connects us with others, lightens our mood, and even has physiological benefits. This chapter explores the importance of building a network of cheerleaders and humor-loving friends who can help you navigate life's ups and downs with a sense of humor, hit the "meh" button when things get tough, and drown out negativity with waves of laughter.

the science of laughter

Laughter, often dismissed as mere frivolity, has profound effects on the human body and mind. When we laugh, our brain releases endorphins, the body's natural feel-good chemicals. These endorphins not only elevate our mood but also reduce stress and pain. Laughter also decreases the levels of stress hormones like cortisol and adrenaline, promoting relaxation and a sense of well-being.

From a social perspective, laughter is a bonding tool. It helps us connect with others, breaking down barriers and fostering a sense of belonging. Shared laughter can create strong social ties and encourage a positive, supportive environment. When you're laughing with friends, you feel less isolated and more capable of handling life's challenges.

the need for cheerleaders

Building a network of cheerleaders—people who support and uplift you—is crucial for maintaining a positive outlook. Cheerleaders aren't just those who praise and applaud; they are individuals who bring humor, perspective, and lightness to your life. They can turn a gloomy day into a bright one with a joke, a funny story, or a shared memory that brings laughter.

In a world filled with stress, negativity, and uncertainty, having a network of cheerleaders can be a lifeline. They remind you not to take things too seriously, to find humor in the everyday, and to laugh at your mistakes. This network can help you hit the "meh" button, allowing you to let go of what doesn't serve you and focus on what brings joy.

building your network of cheerleaders

Building a network of cheerleaders doesn't happen overnight. It requires effort, intention, and a willingness to seek out like-minded individuals who value humor and positivity. Here are steps to help you create this supportive network:

identify the right people:

start by identifying people in your life who share your sense of humor or appreciate a good laugh. These might be friends, family members, colleagues, or even acquaintances who seem to radiate positivity. Look for those who are quick to smile, tell jokes, or find humor in everyday situations.

cultivate relationships:

once you've identified potential cheerleaders, focus on cultivating relationships with them. This involves spending time together, sharing experiences, and engaging in activities that encourage laughter. Invite them to social gatherings, movie nights, or outings where humor is a central theme.

encourage humor:

create an environment that encourages humor and laughter. Share funny videos, memes, or stories that make you laugh. Encourage others to share their own sources of humor, fostering a culture of laughter within your network.

participate in humor-focused activities:

engage in activities that promote laughter and lightheartedness. This might include attending comedy shows, participating in improv classes, or watching humorous movies with friends. These activities can strengthen your network and provide shared experiences that generate laughter.

be authentic:

while building a network of cheerleaders, it's important to be authentic. Don't force humor or try to be someone you're not. The best humor comes from genuine moments and shared experiences. By being yourself, you'll attract people who appreciate you for who you are.

the power of shared laughter

Shared laughter is a unique bonding experience. It creates inside jokes, strengthens relationships, and helps you navigate difficult times with a sense of humor. When you're part of a network of cheerleaders, shared laughter can become a powerful tool for resilience.

Imagine a scenario where you're going through a challenging period at work. Deadlines are looming, stress is high, and mistakes seem to be piling up. In this environment, negativity can easily take over, leading to frustration and burnout. However, if you're part of a network of cheerleaders, they can help you find humor in the chaos. They might share a funny story about their own workplace mishaps, reminding you that everyone makes mistakes. This shared laughter can alleviate stress and provide a much-needed perspective shift.

Similarly, in personal relationships, shared laughter can defuse tension and strengthen bonds. When disagreements arise, humor can act as a bridge, allowing you to reconnect and find common ground. A well-timed joke or a playful remark can turn a heated argument into a moment of shared laughter, reminding both parties that they care about each other.

Using laughter to drown out negativity

Negativity is pervasive, especially in today's world, where bad news and pessimism seem to dominate the headlines. Building a network of cheerleaders can help you drown out this negativity with laughter and positivity. Here's how you can use laughter as a powerful tool against negativity:

reframe negative situations:

when faced with a negative situation, try to reframe it with humor. Instead of dwelling on what's going wrong, find a funny angle or a humorous story that relates to the situation. This reframing can help you shift your focus from negativity to laughter.

create a humor playlist:

compile a playlist of your favorite comedy shows, stand-up specials, or funny movies. When negativity starts to creep in, hit play and let the laughter wash over you. This humor playlist can be a quick and effective way to change your mood.

lean on your cheerleaders:

when you're feeling overwhelmed by negativity, reach out to your network of cheerleaders. Share your concerns and let them bring humor and perspective to the situation. Sometimes, all it takes is a funny text or a quick phone call to lift your spirits.

practice laughter yoga:

laughter yoga is a unique practice that combines deep breathing exercises with intentional laughter. It's designed to reduce stress and promote a sense of well-being. Consider joining a laughter yoga class or practicing at home to incorporate more laughter into your life.

The laughter lifeline is a powerful concept that emphasizes the importance of building a network of cheerleaders and humor-loving friends. This network can help you navigate life's challenges with laughter, perspective, and positivity. By cultivating relationships with those who value humor, you can create a supportive environment that drowns out negativity and brings joy to your life.

As you continue your journey, remember that laughter is a universal language that connects people across boundaries. It has the power to heal, uplift, and transform. By embracing the laughter lifeline, you're taking a significant step toward a more joyful and fulfilling life, surrounded by a network of cheerleaders who make every day a little brighter.

Chapter 12: the final jerk-eviction party:

Celebrate your journey with a humor-filled ritual, like writing a goodbye song to your inner jerk or burning a negativity piñata.

You've reached the final chapter of your book, and what a journey it's been! You've battled inner critics, silenced negative voices, and created a powerful support system. Now it's time to celebrate your triumphs, acknowledge your growth, and, most importantly, have fun doing it. In this chapter, we'll explore ways to throw the ultimate jerk-eviction party, where you say goodbye to your inner jerk and all the negativity it represents. Whether you choose to write a goodbye song, burn a negativity piñata, or create a unique ritual, the key is to infuse the celebration with humor, joy, and a sense of accomplishment.

why celebrate?

Before we dive into party ideas, let's consider why celebrating this milestone is so important. Overcoming your inner jerk is no small feat. It's a journey of self-discovery, growth, and resilience. By celebrating, you acknowledge your progress and create a positive anchor for future challenges. A well-planned celebration can also inspire others who are on their own journey to overcome negativity.

Celebrations are powerful markers that signal the end of one chapter and the beginning of another. They allow you to reflect on your accomplishments, connect with supportive friends and family, and set the tone for the next phase of your life. By turning the eviction of your inner jerk into a festive event, you create lasting memories and solidify the positive changes you've made.

planning your jerk-eviction party

Every great party starts with careful planning. Here's a step-by-step guide to help you organize your jerk-eviction party, ensuring it's a memorable and joyous occasion.

step 1: set your intentions

Begin by setting your intentions for the party. What do you hope to achieve? Perhaps you want to mark the end of a difficult chapter, celebrate your newfound confidence, or simply have fun with friends and family. Your intentions will guide the rest of your planning.

Consider what aspects of your journey you'd like to highlight during the party. For example, if you've written a goodbye song to your inner jerk, you might want to perform it or play it during the celebration. If you're burning a negativity piñata, think about what it represents and how you want to symbolize your victory over negativity.

step 2: choose a location

The location you choose will set the stage for your party. If you have a large group of friends and family, consider hosting the event at a community center, park, or rented venue. For smaller gatherings, a backyard or living room can work just as well. The key is to create a space where everyone feels comfortable and where you can carry out your planned activities.

step 3: invite your support network

Your jerk-eviction party is a time to gather with those who have supported you throughout your journey. Make a list of the friends, family, and mentors who have been there for you, and send them invitations. You can get creative with the invitations, using humor or references to your journey. For example, you could send out "eviction notices" to your inner jerk, letting your guests know that they're invited to the eviction party.

step 4: plan the activities

The activities you choose will be the heart of your party. Here are some ideas to get you started:

- **goodbye song**: write a song or a poem to bid farewell to your inner jerk. You can perform it live, play a recording, or have everyone sing along. This activity is not only fun but also cathartic, allowing you to express your journey creatively.

- **negativity piñata**: fill a piñata with symbols of negativity—such as pieces of paper with negative thoughts, or small items that represent past struggles—and let everyone take turns hitting it. As the piñata breaks open, it's a symbolic release of negativity, and the treats inside can represent the positivity you're embracing.

- **journaling station**: set up a station with journals and pens where guests can write down their own experiences with inner critics or negative thoughts.

This activity can encourage sharing and reflection, allowing everyone to connect on a deeper level.

- **laughter games**: include games and activities that promote laughter and joy. Consider games like "cards against humanity," "apples to apples," or a good old-fashioned round of charades. The goal is to create a lighthearted atmosphere where everyone can have fun.

step 5: create a positive atmosphere

Decorate your party space with uplifting and humorous elements. Use bright colors, positive quotes, and images that evoke happiness. You could create a "wall of positivity" where guests can write encouraging messages or share their favorite moments from your journey.

Music is also a key component of a positive atmosphere. Create a playlist of upbeat songs that inspire joy and energy. You can even include songs that have personal significance to your journey, adding a layer of nostalgia and meaning to the celebration.

step 6: express gratitude

During your party, take a moment to express gratitude to those who have supported you. This can be a brief speech, a toast, or a simple thank-you to each person. Acknowledging the people who have been there for you is an important part of the celebration, reinforcing the connections that have helped you overcome your inner jerk.

the ritual of closure

A jerk-eviction party is more than just a fun gathering; it's a ritual of closure. By creating a humor-filled ritual, you give yourself permission to let go of the past and embrace the future. This ritual can take many forms, but the common thread is a sense of finality and release.

Consider creating a symbolic act that represents the eviction of your inner jerk. It could be the burning of a letter where you've written out all the negative thoughts and beliefs you want to leave behind. Or you could release balloons with words of encouragement and positivity, letting them soar into the sky as a symbol of your new beginning.

The ritual of closure is a powerful way to mark the end of your journey and the beginning of a new chapter. It allows you to put closure to the struggles you've overcome and step confidently into the future.

beyond the jerk-eviction party

While the jerk-eviction party is a significant milestone, it's important to remember that your journey doesn't end here. The inner critic may try to make a comeback, and new challenges will arise. However, the party serves as a reminder of your strength, resilience, and ability to overcome negativity with humor and positivity.

As you move forward, continue to build on the relationships you've cultivated, maintain your network of cheerleaders, and find humor in everyday life. The tools and techniques you've learned throughout your journey will continue to serve you well.

The final jerk-eviction party is a celebration of your growth, resilience, and determination. It's an opportunity to acknowledge your journey, connect with supportive friends and family, and have fun in the process. By creating a humor-filled ritual, you can symbolically evict your inner jerk and embrace a brighter, more positive future.

As you celebrate, remember that laughter is a powerful tool for healing and connection. It has the power to transform even the darkest moments into opportunities for growth and joy. By infusing your party with laughter, you're not just celebrating the end of one chapter—you're setting the stage for a future filled with positivity and laughter.

Bonus chapter

THE INNER JERK'S GUIDE to sabotaging your happiness

welcome to the inner jerk's school of misery

Hello, ladies and gentlemen, trolls, goblins, and inner critics of all shapes and sizes! Welcome to the "inner jerk's guide to sabotaging your happiness." i'm your host, debbie downer dave, and today i'm going to walk you through some foolproof ways to keep yourself perpetually miserable. Forget those self-help books that talk about growth and transformation—i'm here to make sure you're firmly grounded in the muck of despair and self-sabotage. Let's dive in, shall we?

step 1: comparison is key

If you really want to stay miserable, the best thing you can do is compare yourself to others. And i don't mean just a little comparison—i mean full-on, soul-crushing, "why am i not as successful, attractive, wealthy, or talented as [insert celebrity name here]?" kind of comparison. Social media is your best friend here. Follow everyone who seems to be living their best life and make sure to internalize that you're a complete and utter failure by comparison. You're welcome.

step 2: neglect self-care

If there's one thing that can quickly lead you down the path of misery, it's neglecting self-care. Don't exercise. Don't sleep. Definitely don't eat anything that might be considered healthy. Who needs a balanced diet when you can have pizza for breakfast, lunch, and dinner? The key here is to create a cycle of fatigue and lethargy that will keep you from ever feeling good about yourself. It's science.

step 3: dwell on past mistakes

When it comes to self-sabotage, there's no better fuel than past mistakes. Make sure to replay your biggest blunders on a loop in your mind. Never let yourself forget that time you tripped in front of your crush or sent that embarrassing email to your boss. Keep those memories fresh and use them as a reminder that you're a walking disaster. The past is your best source of misery—don't let it go to waste.

step 4: always assume the worst

If you're not living in constant fear of the future, you're doing it wrong. Always assume the worst-case scenario is just around the corner. You got a new job? It's probably going to end in failure. Met someone interesting? They're likely plotting your demise. Whatever you do, don't ever entertain the idea that things might go well. Optimism is for chumps.

step 5: overcommit and overwhelm

One surefire way to keep yourself in a state of perpetual stress and misery is to overcommit. Say "yes" to everything. Overbook your schedule and then watch as the anxiety builds. Bonus points if you forget important deadlines and have to scramble to meet them at the last minute. The goal is to create an environment where you're constantly on edge, never quite catching up with everything you need to do. It's a recipe for disaster, which is precisely the point.

step 6: isolate yourself

Social isolation is the cherry on top of the misery sundae. Make sure to avoid friends, family, and anyone else who might try to cheer you up. Tell yourself that no one understands you, and make sure to decline any social invitations that come your way. If you're feeling particularly ambitious, go ahead and burn some bridges. Ghosting people is a great way to ensure you have a lonely existence.

step 7: reject help and advice

Finally, if someone offers you advice or help, dismiss it immediately. You don't need their positivity or constructive criticism—you're perfectly fine wallowing in your own misery, thank you very much. Reject any attempt at intervention and make it clear that you're in control of your own unhappiness. Keep repeating the mantra, "i don't need your help," until it becomes second nature.

frequently asked jerk-eviction questions

the inner jerk faq: your guide to silencing your inner critic

Welcome to the "frequently asked jerk-eviction questions" section of our guide. I'm your host, debbie downer dave, and i'm here to address some of the most common concerns and anxieties about silencing your inner critic. Remember, folks, if you start feeling better about yourself, i'm out of a job, so let's proceed with caution. Nevertheless, here are some questions and answers to help you deal with your inner jerk—or at least tolerate them with a sense of humor.

question 1: how do i identify my inner jerk?

Your inner jerk, also known as your inner critic, is that little voice in your head that tells you you're not good enough, smart enough, or worthy of happiness. If you've ever caught yourself saying, "i can't do this," or "i'm such a failure," that's your inner jerk talking. To identify your inner jerk, just listen for the sound of constant negativity. If you hear it, congratulations—you've found your inner critic! Don't worry; you're not alone.

question 2: can i get rid of my inner jerk entirely?

Oh, bless your heart. You want to get rid of your inner jerk entirely? Good luck with that. Your inner jerk is like that annoying relative who shows up uninvited to every family gathering. They just won't leave. But the good news is, you don't have to get rid of them entirely to have a happy life. You just need to learn how to manage them and turn down their volume. Think of it like learning to live with a loud neighbor. Earplugs are your friend.

question 3: what's the best way to deal with my inner jerk?

Humor. I'm not kidding (and i rarely kid). If you can laugh at your inner jerk, you're halfway to silencing them. When your inner critic starts ranting about how you're bound to fail, respond with, "oh, thanks for the pep talk, negative nancy. I'll keep that in mind while i go and live my life." by using humor, you take away some of the inner jerk's power and remind yourself that you don't have to take everything they say seriously. Laughter is the best eviction notice.

question 4: can i ever be completely happy with my inner jerk around?

Ah, the age-old question: can you be happy when your inner jerk is constantly nagging at you? The answer is, yes, you can. But remember, happiness is not about having a perfect life or being free from all negativity. It's about learning to embrace the messiness and find joy despite your inner jerk's best efforts to bring you down. It's like going to a circus—the clowns are scary, but the trapeze artists are amazing. Focus on the trapeze artists.

question 5: what should i do if my inner jerk is really loud?

If your inner jerk is blasting negativity like a foghorn, it's time to call in the reinforcements. Surround yourself with positive people, read uplifting books, and engage in activities that make you happy. You might even want to try meditation or mindfulness to quiet the noise. The goal is to drown out the inner jerk's voice with positivity and support. And if all else fails, just put on some noise-canceling headphones and dance it out. Trust me, it helps.

question 6: is it okay to talk back to my inner jerk?

Absolutely! Talking back to your inner jerk is not only okay; it's highly encouraged. When your inner critic tells you you're not good enough, respond with something like, "thanks for the input, captain buzzkill, but i've got this." by talking back, you're asserting your own self-worth and setting boundaries with your inner jerk. Just be careful not to engage in a full-blown argument—you'll never win. Keep it short and sassy, and then move on.

question 7: how can i keep my inner jerk from sabotaging my happiness?

The best way to keep your inner jerk from sabotaging your happiness is to stay one step ahead. Practice self-compassion, take care of yourself, and focus on the things that bring you joy. Create a positive environment, set realistic goals, and don't be afraid to seek help from others when you need it. And remember, your inner jerk thrives on negativity, so keep the positive vibes flowing. The happier you are, the more your inner jerk will take a back seat.

The "shut up, brain" self-help revolution

turning the tables on your inner critic

We've covered a lot of ground, folks. From embracing the inner jerk to finding humor in the chaos, we've journeyed through the dark, twisty corridors of negativity and come out on the other side with a few chuckles and a lighter heart. Now, let's take a moment to reflect on what we've learned and how we can apply it to our everyday lives.

the power of humor

Humor is your secret weapon against the inner jerk. When you're feeling overwhelmed or discouraged, a good laugh can work wonders. It breaks the tension, reminds you not to take yourself too seriously, and helps you see the lighter side of things. So, the next time your inner critic starts spouting nonsense, find something funny to focus on—whether it's a hilarious meme, a goofy joke, or just your own absurdity. Laughter is like kryptonite to the inner jerk.

embracing imperfection

One of the biggest traps set by the inner jerk is the pursuit of perfection. If you're always striving to be flawless, you're setting yourself up for disappointment. Instead, embrace imperfection and understand that life is messy, unpredictable, and full of surprises. When you accept that you're not perfect and that's okay, you take away the inner jerk's favorite weapon. It's like deflating their balloon—suddenly, they don't have as much power.

self-compassion and kindness

Self-compassion is the antidote to self-criticism. When you treat yourself with kindness and understanding, you create a barrier against the inner jerk's negativity. Practice self-compassion by speaking to yourself as you would a good friend. Give yourself permission to make mistakes, learn from them, and keep going. And remember, you deserve the same compassion you would give to others. It's not selfish—it's essential for your well-being.

building a support system

No one can go it alone, especially when battling an inner jerk. Build a support system of friends, family, and loved ones who uplift and encourage you. Surround yourself with people who believe in you, and don't be afraid to lean on them when you need a boost. Your inner jerk thrives on isolation, so the more connected you are, the less power they have. It's like assembling a team of inner-jerk busters—together, you're unstoppable.

living authentically

Finally, the best way to shut up your brain and silence your inner critic is to live authentically. Embrace who you are, quirks and all, and don't try to fit into someone else's mold. When you live according to your values and pursue the things that bring you joy, you're telling the inner jerk to take a hike. Authenticity is like an invisibility cloak—the inner jerk can't see you when you're being true to yourself.

conclusion: a lighter, happier path

Congratulations, brave reader, for making it through this journey with debbie downer dave as your guide. We've explored the depths of self-sabotage and climbed the peaks of self-compassion, all while keeping a sense of humor. Now, as you move forward, remember that your inner jerk doesn't have the final say in your happiness. You do. Use humor, self-compassion, and the support of others to create a life that brings you joy. And if the inner jerk tries to sneak back in, just tell them to "shut up, brain"—you've got this.

Thanks for joining me on this adventure, and remember, happiness is a choice—just make sure to choose it with a smile. Now go forth and conquer your inner jerk with laughter, positivity, and a whole lot of "meh." the revolution has begun!